The Scientifically Proven Reality
of Life After Death

Written by Russell Symonds
(Yogi Shaktivirya)

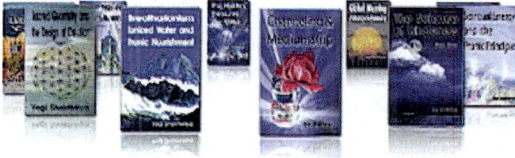

Copyright Information

Table of Contents:

Summary of Book:

Introduction: Science Rejects the Afterlife as Being a "Fairy Story"

Part 1 - Scientific Proof and Personal Experiences

1.1 - Here Are Four Scientifically Proven Out-of-Body Experiences

1.2 - My Search for Truth and Personal Experiences from the Afterlife

Part 2 - Leslie Flint's Direct Voice Mediumship

2.1 - Leslie Flint: An Inconvenient Truth for Christian Theologians and Skeptical Scientists

2.2 - Leslie Flint's Impossible Powers: Why Did He Not Make Millions as a Parlor Trick Showman?

2.3 - BadPsychics.com Forum Administration/Members Hate my Information!

2.4 - Leslie's "Etheric" Guests Never Coughed or Sputtered

2.5 - Messages From the Afterlife - How the Paranormal Voices Came Through

Part 3 - Life in the Astral Worlds

3.1 - The Exciting Reality of it All

3.2 - An Absolutely Natural, Complete and Profoundly Fulfilling Existence

3.3 - The Colors Are Far More Vivid, Extensive and Varied

3.4 - Eating and Sleeping in the Afterlife

3.5 - Afterlife Interests, Skills and Hobbies

Introduction

Materialistic Science Rejects the Afterlife as Being a "Fairy Story"

It is most unfortunate that the official viewpoint of mainstream science is that there is no afterlife. A recent statement by renowned physicist Stephen Hawking says that heaven is "a fairy story" for those afraid of death. When the brain shuts down, he assumes, all the senses stop working and all experiencing ceases forever. While assuming we are nothing more than physical computers, he states, "There is no heaven or afterlife for broken down computers." Conventional science even goes as far as to assume that all near-death experiences are simply the hallucinations of a dying brain.

Long before finding my own proof of the afterlife, I used to find such conclusions by science not only profoundly depressing, but absolutely terrifying. What a horrible and lonely feeling it must be to assume that all one's deceased loved ones are simply gone forever and then realizing you too (often after a long struggle with a disease or illness) will simply cease to exist one day! It is impossible to even imagine ceasing to exist and not ever having consciousness any more, especially in the view of the fact that physical life is already terribly hard, unfair and difficult for nearly everyone, even Stephen Hawking, who was diagnosed with Lou Gehrig's disease at the age of 21.

However, we can thank the Universe that the truth is always far stranger than fiction and far more merciful and complex than any pre-conclusions drawn by even the greatest of scientists! I know for certain there is far more to life than what is perceived on the surface. I am surprised that Stephen Hawking never acknowledged the incredible organization and infinite complexity of nature and the quantum field of ever-expanding space itself as evidence of the existence of a universally aware intelligence or multidimensional Creative Principle which we are all a part of.

The universe contains many surprises yet to be discovered. Did you know that the overwhelming majority of the material in the universe is made up of something called "dark matter" that astronomers don't even fully understand? And then there is dark energy, which is even more mysterious!

Some of the latest studies on consciousness done by scientists such as Dean Radin, Ph. D, have shown that awareness is definitely not limited to the physical brain as Stephen Hawking has assumed, and is not even dependent on its existence! The brain, rather than a producer of consciousness, seems to be more like a channel of information to and from an individual aspect of a universal quantum field of consciousness.

Having been blessed with an experience myself of consciousness (remote viewing) beyond my physical brain and physical senses, I know this is true! One time during meditation around 2006, I saw something happening 50 meters away from my apartment! I saw a vision of roofers working around several structures on a roof. An hour later as I walked through an alley to check my mail box, I saw the exact same thing: there was some construction work going on at a neighbor's house: a new roof was being built. I was utterly astonished by the scene of workers walking around the chimneys and other structures on the roof just like I'd seen earlier in my vision!

Part 1 - Scientific Proof and Personal Experiences

1.1 - Here Are Four Scientifically Proven Out-of-Body Experiences

I keep seeing so often in so many forums, science articles, etc. that astral projection and life after death has never been scientifically proven. This assumption is simply not true! Just do a little research and you will find countless cases scientifically confirming the existence of a life beyond the physical clearly demonstrating over and over that consciousness is definitely not limited to the dimensions and/or lifespan of the human brain.

I studied other people's life after death experiences long enough to safely say that I am stuck no more with simply a "belief" in the afterlife, instead I enjoy a rather definite "knowing" that death is a great lie and not at all the final ending so many materialistic doctors and scientists would have us believe! Some of the best evidence comes from a large number of near-death experiences when the person was able to see and hear actual scenes that were later verified by doctors, researchers and scientists. Here are four scientifically proven well documented famous cases of actual out-of-body experiences:

1) There was a lady by the name of Maria who during a

cardiac arrest, floated above the roof of a hospital and noted the precise details and whereabouts of a tennis shoe (with one of its laces tucked under and worn out at the area of its "big toe") stuck on the edge of a ledge. Later, her nurse, Kimberly Clark Sharp (author of "Beyond the LIght"), found that tennis shoe on the roof exactly as described by Maria.

2) Then there is the fascinating case of Vicky Noratuk who, completely blind from birth, could actually see during her NDE. After a serious car accident in 1973, Vicky saw many vivid scenes from outside her physical body in the hospital and of the afterlife where she saw and recognized her friends Debby and Diane who already passed over several years ago. After she recovered she was able to clearly recall some of the events and conversation that took place in the hospital, the appearance of her physical body, and exactly how it was damaged.

3) There was also a lady by the name of Pam Reynolds (singer) who while having no brain activity whatsoever and no blood flowing at all through her brain, and with a body temperature lowered to 60 degrees F, could see from a viewpoint outside her body and floated around the room. She vividly and clearly recalled all the clinical details of her brain surgery and heard some of the conversation, even though she wore ear plugs taped over

her ears with a beeping sound. All her details and conversations were later confirmed.

4) A young, unmarried woman by the name of "Miss Z" from Southern California was the subject of a laboratory study by psychic researcher Charles T. Tart originally published in the "Journal of the American Society for Psychical Research," 1968, vol. 62, no. 1, pp. 3-27. Miss Z claimed to undergo several spontaneous out of body experiences per week and was observed in Tart's sleep laboratory for four non-consecutive nights over a period of two months. Her movements were well controlled and carefully monitored while attached to multiple physiological recording devices such as two EEG channels and one REM channel, etc. A piece of paper with a clearly written unique five-digit random number was left on a small shelf five and a half feet above the subject's head every night after the woman was ready to fall asleep. At the end of the fourth night, she correctly called out the target number, 25132. With the odds of correctly guessing such a number being 1 in 100,000, I would have to say this is pretty strong evidence that her OOBEs were actual!

The above four are just a small sample of the vast research done on the out-of-body and near-death experiences encountered by millions of people every year.

Nearly every case is quite dramatic and most definitely not simply the artifacts of a dying, hallucinating brain. Many scientists throughout history also came to the firm conclusion that there is life after death. Here is just a few of them: Allan Kardec, Esq., Dr. Alfred Russel Wallace, Sir William Crookes, The Rev. William Stainton Moses, Sir Oliver Lodge, Sir Arthur Conan Doyle, Dr. William James, The Rev. Charles Drayton Thomas, Dr. Hereward Carrington, Dr. Harry Price, and Elisabeth Kübler-Ross, M.D. and many, many more.

The most spectacular evidence I have ever found yet in my entire life is the collection of over three hundred paranormal voice recordings (lasting from 10 to 55 minutes each) in the presence of the direct voice medium Leslie Flint (1911-1994).

Leslie Flint must have been the most tried, proven and tested medium of the 20th century, without anyone, over a period of 60 years, ever being able to disprove him or expose him as a fraud. First-hand experiences of Leslie Flint's seances forced skeptics to either give up their world view or try to make something up to have it seem as if it was anything other than the actual paranormal voices that could be clearly heard throughout the darkened seance room!

Much verifiable and extremely vital information came through Leslie Flint. The messages that came through Leslie Flint and related sources of information will be the main subject of this book.

1.2 - My Search for Truth and Personal Experiences from the Afterlife

Not knowing enough about the afterlife, I was at first quite skeptical regarding most of the available information out there, but very interested and hopeful that somehow there could be a way to not only prove the existence of an afterlife, but also to find ways that communication could be established with those who have passed over. I therefore studied the subject for over 36 years and listened with immense interest to hundreds of meaningful paranormal voice recordings from some well-known direct voice mediums and read hundreds of near-death and astral projection experiences.

The only way I know of to explain all this phenomenal evidence is there must be realms beyond the physical (perhaps consisting of dark matter), and from what I learned, the physical is one of the most dismal, limited and difficult realms. Every day while in this most limited and difficult condition called physical life, I simply can't imagine there not being an afterlife!

I am not religious, I am spiritual; there is a vast difference between the spiritual, material and religious aspects of human thought. The material and religious aspects separate man from the reality of the afterlife in all manner of ways resulting in a great deal of darkness, emotional pain and confusion. In my early years I felt this emotional pain and horrible emptiness so succinctly that I began a lifelong and serious search for spiritual awareness through meditation and yoga nearly 40 years ago and eventually experienced some amazing phenomena.

In my early twenties in the fall of 1979, while falling asleep during a deep meditative state I was "pulled" out of my body into a white area where I could vividly recognize someone from one of my college classes sitting in front of me. I found out later he had just died in a serious motorcycle accident!

While sleeping completely alone in my room around Christmas time in 1991, over a week after my mother passed away, something tapped on my left shoulder rather vigorously causing me to awaken very suddenly in shock and amazement! However, no one was there in my room to be seen but I could have sworn there was a disembodied hand there!

Many years later, sometime in May of 2009, while fast

asleep during the early morning hours, I experienced a "dream" of being lifted out of my body by many spirits into an immense cavern of volcanic rock with a sandy bottom. I could feel their hands pulling me out of my body and then giving me a tour of a tiny portion of what they would consider to be their world in the afterlife.

I shook hands with many spirits or souls bathed in a warm light and clothed in very casual, light attire such as pajamas and Hawaiian shirts, and we all sat down together in a naturally constructed amphitheater to enjoy a concert involving unusual musical instruments and strange but highly uplifting and therapeutic music I never heard before.

In another unforgettable "dream" three months later on August of 2009, I found myself floating up out of my apartment and on to the roof top where new landscapes in the sky opened up before me revealing streams, parklands, hills, mountains and fields with numerous dwellings and communities! I had an adventure of a lifetime walking up pathways, bridges and trees I never saw before with the intent to meet one of the dwellers inside one of the houses (built from the natural tan-colored earthen materials surrounding it) to find out what "daily" astral life is like.

I met a person who I felt familiar with and he showed the inside of his house which looked so similar to the ones on Earth. I even drank from his tap water and will never forget the taste of that pure, clean sparkling and living "astral" water that came out of his "astral" faucet!

More details of some of the above "astral" experiences can be found in the section on astral projection toward the end of my book.

If I were not 100% certain about the existence of the afterlife, I would not at all feel inclined to write about something that does not exist. I am also aware of various energies beyond what mainstream science would simply dismiss as imagination or worse. I experience levels of energy (prana) beyond the physical all the time. I am a yogi living a pure, chaste life and as long as certain conditions are met, I live in a state of bliss! I meditated since the age of 14 and in spite of numerous personal set-backs, dedicated my whole life to Spirit. Spirit is the source of my greatest love and happiness.

Part 2 - Leslie Flint's Direct Voice Mediumship

2.1 - Leslie Flint: An Inconvenient Truth for Christian Theologians and Skeptical Scientists

There are so many individuals alive today still wondering whether there is life after death, and if there is, what sort of afterlife is it? How can one be sure of the information available today on such controversial subjects as this one? I studied all aspects of this subject quite seriously and as a skeptic since 1972.

Unfortunately there has been much misinformation on this subject floating around throughout history, mostly created by powerful priests, popes and bishops trying to keep the masses under their control. I have only recently found some sources of information that I can trust such as the near-death experiences of others, my own personal experiences, and the awesome **Leslie Flint Educational Trust** recordings.

One can visit **The Leslie Flint Educational Trust** website for a massive collection of absolutely genuine and lengthy (some lasting up to 50 minutes) paranormal voice recordings taped by George Woods, Betty Greene and many others from the mid 1950's to early 1990's. After extremely carefully analyzing all their work and all other recordings, I have to say, they are the most substantial breakthrough evidence in afterlife research ever.

At the Leslie Flint website, one can listen to an introductory message by one of Mr. Leslie Flint's main seance members and tape recording specialists, Betty Greene, and there are recordings of radio programs, lectures, etc. explaining direct voice mediumship, and interviews with Leslie Flint which can also be found on the Leslie Flint Trust website, www.LeslieFlint.com.

It is best to keep an open mind and try to avoid any preconceived ideas, notions, and misconceptions, because direct voice mediumship is a serious, delicate and intricate subject that very few understand or even take seriously. The dramatically varying paranormal voices have to go through several stages of thought to etheric to sound translation through the intermediary of ectoplasm before they can be physically heard and then recorded on tapes of varying quality. The original personalities, information, and various accents often come through extremely well and usually sounding very similar to how the person sounded while still alive.

Many of the personalities that come through are often channeled through a spirit much closer to the Earth vibration, because the levels of vibration or spheres that they come from are often too far removed (out of range) from the vibrational level of the voice box. Rather like a relay system with Leslie Flint being the physical medium or channel on Earth, while possibly the spirit guide Dr. Marshall, and spirit control, "Mickey" (John Whitehead who passed away at age 11 near beginning of the 20th century) provides the mediumship on the etheric level.

Spirits from much higher spheres can then communicate, however some of their original voice is lost. This is why many of the souls from the higher spheres may sometimes sound similar to Dr. Marshall or Mickey. The overall process is tricky and extremely complex. The astonishing thing is that we are able to hear anything at all, and that anyone in the world with a computer and an internet connection can now listen to a huge selection of them!

Still skeptical? It is an overwhelming tendency even among the most brilliant and professional scientific minds to completely dismiss a subject such as alien visitations or afterlife as completely false long before knowing anything about it. Such prejudice and ignorance is like the child who naively declares that science is completely false without first carefully understanding what science and the scientific method really are all about in the first place.

Those who in a closed-minded way condemn a subject solely based on what far too little they know about it already are indeed ignorant in the worst way. "Condemnation without investigation" kills knowledge. I also find the long held, dark age Christian belief that spiritualism is the "devil's work" equally irksome, absolutely non-scientific and frustrating. When it comes to realization of truth, especially regarding the afterlife, humankind has been extremely poor at it.

Mr. Leslie Flint (1911-1994) has to be one of the most authentic, most closely scrutinized, and verifiable sources of afterlife information ever, and was one of the most prolific mediums of the 20th century and the most thoroughly tested. I will explain to you why I think there is no way these voices could have been a hoax and why I am 100% convinced that the information that came through is real, verifiable and precise! You will see why it would be more incredible that they were somehow faked than actually be real souls speaking through in the candid, honest, from-the-heart, natural and casual manner that they had spoken in.

After very carefully listening to over 200 recordings (out of a collection of one thousand old tape recordings most of which are not yet available on the internet and taped by George Woods, Betty Greene and others from the late

1950's to early 1990's) and many more recently released, I can with 100% certainty guarantee that all of the recordings are of absolutely genuine people claiming to be dead! The whole effect is simply impossible to reproduce fraudulently.

One would need numerous impossibly talented child and adult actors and actresses just to recreate these tapes without copying them! Quite ordinary and natural-sounding disembodied personalities have been caught on tape! Regardless of the fact they were spirits or not, they were definitely real, sincere, honest-to-goodness-sounding people claiming to be spirits from another existence, and definitely NOT actors and definitely NOT those attempting to contrive or fraudulently represent spirits.

You must listen to all of the recordings carefully yourself to fully understand exactly what I mean and why I know they are genuine; by how the personalities presented themselves, how they sounded, the descriptions they conveyed, how they conversed very intelligently with the sitters, how they answered questions only the person would know, how some seemed to be able to read the sitter's mind(s), how some were able to see things going in a completely darkened room and recount the events of the day only the sitter had known about, the 100%

meaningful and inspiring spiritual subject matter and wisdom they eloquently expressed, their unique mannerisms, the heartfelt reunions of old friendships and loved ones, their genuine sense of humor and funny, eccentric quirks, the difficulties some had communicating, the limitations they faced, the odd and unusual effects caused by the ectoplasm they were using, the different accents, foreign and/or long forgotten dead languages and songs, and how they concluded their talks, etc.

Even if somehow the voices were faked, how on this Earth would Leslie Flint get hundreds of 100% honest-sounding actors and actresses to spontaneously come through out of thin air and correctly answer all questions from sitters and from audiences as large as two thousand people in lecture halls and theaters (such as Kingsway Hall) throughout the UK? Countless correct names and addresses of dead relatives were given, including countless details only the living individuals addressed would know about. If they were faked, where would all the "psychically gifted" (they would have to be to correctly provide details known only to the sitters) actors and actresses needed to answer all the questions come from?

Then who paid all these actors and actresses to create these highly relevant and intelligent conversations with complete strangers for over a period of sixty years, even answering questions sometimes just before they were asked as if they were reading one's mind and then often speaking at length about the importance of unconditional love, forgiveness, honesty, humanity, service to others and an all-embracing "Christianity" without and bias, judgement or dogma? If somehow all these voices were faked, we would be left with more questions than answers.

2.2 - Leslie Flint's "Impossible" Powers: Why Did He Not Make Millions as a Parlor Trick Showman?

Because of the extraordinary nature of Leslie Flint's "powers," there are still many, many people who do not accept or believe in what he had achieved. Somehow they are not convinced enough in spite of the recordings, the overwhelming evidence, the information that came through, and all the witnesses who were in themselves definitely convinced. What I have found regarding nonbelievers, is they usually had the following attitudes in common: a strong prejudice or conviction in their negative opinion of Leslie Flint, poor information or knowledge in general about the subject of spiritualism and spiritism, no personal spiritual or psychic experiences of any sort, an overall lack of open-mindedness, and finally an inability or unwillingness to fully investigate the possibility of the afterlife. Often it is one's religious beliefs that get in the way of allowing a more compassionate and understanding approach to the validity and innocence of spiritualism, or it is often due to an opposite view steeped in atheism and an overwhelmingly materialistic and mechanical view of life.

Let's assume that somehow Leslie Flint was just a fraud, I don't know how he could have fooled everyone who attended his seances for 60 years, and he would have to be a magician many times more subtle than Chris Angel combined with the wisdom of King Solomon and the insight and psychic power of Edgar Cayce along with a photographic memory and an unusually creative and consistent imagination!

If he really was just a stunning and ingenious parlor trick showman as the skeptics would want you to believe, then why did he not simply perform as an incredibly unusual magician and/or ventriloquist for a multimillion dollar income at places like Las Vegas? Or why did Leslie Flint, the so-called parlor trick showman, not acquire a multimillion contract with Hollywood or Walt Disney Productions? Instead, why did he leave his beloved dance partner, Gladys and successful dancing career only to be an oftentimes broke direct voice medium spiritualist mocked by skeptics, condemned by devil-phobic, closed-minded Christians, and then bound, gagged and intimately scrutinized repeatedly for years and years by skeptical scientists, doctors and researchers?

The only way I could imagine it being a parlor trick (and it would have to be the most elaborate one ever in the history of humankind to have convinced so many people for 60 years of scrutiny and then never be exposed as a fraud) one would either need some sort of two-way high fidelity quadri-phonic radio (because the voices often could be heard moving in mid-air all around the room!) along with a hidden studio to hide away all the different personalities coming through and then imagine trying to do this in the 1930's, 40's, etc., (with what little technology available then) and with none or little financial support. Leslie Flint was relatively poor throughout most of his life especially when others first discovered his mediumship.

Assuming no electronic equipment was used and yet it was somehow still some sort of magician's trick, Leslie Flint would obviously need some very clever trap doors, hidden hallways, vents, ropes, pulleys, etc. prepared for his "actors and actresses" ahead of time everywhere he went to hold a seance which was often in many public locations throughout the UK or more personal seance rooms that could not have possibly been "rigged" ahead of time as these were all carefully scrutinized before any event.

Obviously Leslie Flint would need quite a team of very stealthy accomplices with him at all times and all of them would have to be somehow paid for, and then always be extremely well informed regarding anyone attending beforehand whose names would often not be known until the beginning of the seance when Leslie Flint's Cockney spirit control "Mickey" announced them! And if his mediumship was faked, where are all the accomplices today? How is it that not one person has yet come forward to say they had been asked or employed by Leslie Flint to fraudulently mimic a huge number of different personalities?

How did Leslie Flint's always incredibly sharp and hilariously witty Cockney control known as "Mickey" in the spirit world (was actually John Whitehead who sold newspapers outside Camden Town, UK until he was killed by a truck when he was eleven) keep the same inimitable, young, childlike voice and same unique personality for so many decades? Mickey's Cockney accent and extraordinary unique characteristics show up regularly in the seance tapes which can be heard online at the Leslie Flint Educational Trust website. Mickey's Cockney accent has extraordinary characteristics. Even the casual listener of one of these tapes should sense that Mickey is indeed a genuine, true-to-life person (in fact a natural comedian) having genuine conversations!

How were those who came through able to correctly answer any questions from anyone in an audience? How did they convince so many people (including lawyers, governors, industrialists and members of royalty sometimes arriving as surprise guests for private seances) they were their dead comrades, relatives and/or loved ones? And before you say "ventriloquist" how could the voices continue to sound perfectly normal and move around the room even while Leslie Flint's mouth was gagged with colored liquid in his mouth and bound to a chair and no one else could be felt or seen in the room? And when he was not gagged, then why was Leslie Flint's voice, coughing, etc. often heard simultaneously along with the spirit's voices in the tapes?

Even though a few materialistic skeptic debunkers desperately tried to discredit Leslie Flint, not one person throughout the 60 years of his mediumship could find any hard evidence whatsoever of any cheating or conjuring. Finally after months of extremely careful observation, one skeptic concluded that the voices had to have emanated from inside his abdomen and another concluded it had to be some form of mass hypnosis or hallucination! Is that possible? Could he have swallowed a 1930's two-way wireless device with a hypnotic effect and quadraphonic voice output?

I would love to see how the world-famous skeptical debunker magician James Randi try to explain all this! He dares not because he cannot. The best he could do is come up with another hard-to-swallow explanation as ridiculous as the gastrointestinal radio or mass hypnosis. (No wonder I get indigestion sometimes while listening to some of these debunkers!) Even then, who or what would have provided all the personalities and information that came through? And then why would Leslie Flint commit hours and hours of his valuable time nearly every week of his life and go to such incredibly eccentric and absurd lengths just to "conjure up the dead" when Mr. Flint was already quite content in his twenties to be a dance instructor and award-winning professional dancer with his beloved dance partner, Gladys?

2.3 - Materialistic Skeptics Hated my Afterlife Information!

The "Bad Psychics" website administration and members, for example, hated my website, especially my positive evaluations of Leslie Flint. It is because all the "evidence" I am presenting naturally clashes against the world views of those who cannot possibly accept the existence of unusual "unproven" phenomena such as ectoplasm and other exotic states of matter such as astral or dark matter.

Spiritualism is just too far outside of the box of their traditional way of thinking and therefore makes them very uncomfortable. I can also be quite skeptical and would not accept anything myself unless there was adequate evidence to support it. I first had to spend thirty-six years of critical research and analysis of countless books, videos, personal experiences and other such material before I was fully convinced of an afterlife.

The "Bad Psychics" website is one of the most "skeptic" websites (authored by those who obviously had no direct experiences of true mediumship, near-death experiences, after death communications, etc.) I have ever seen and people need to be highly critical of anything before accepting it as real anyway. In fact I would be concerned if no one was at first skeptical in one's approach to any new and unusual phenomenon. Therefore, I have no problem with those who are still skeptical as long as they remain compassionately open-minded and are tolerant of those who claim to have experienced paranormal phenomena.

The "Bad Psychics" website administration's "evidence" against Leslie Flint is that Mahatma Gandhi's voice sounds different from when he was alive. Imagine dying and of course having to leave one's physical vocal cords behind to either be cremated or buried along with the body and then having to come back as a spirit talking through someone else's ectoplasm in the form of an artificial "voice box" wouldn't you sound different or at least a little hoarse and even possibly quite similar to many other spirits having to use the same ectoplasmic voice box? Not only that, Gandhi's level of vibration is most likely an extremely high vibration far removed from the Earth's vibration, and most likely another spirit much closer to the Earth's vibration had to have been present to act as an "astral" medium or channel sensitive enough to pick up Gandhi's thoughts yet still low enough in vibration to express through the "voice box." The whole process is anything but simple. Under these conditions, it is an enchanting miracle that anything like Gandhi's voice or accent comes through at all!

Who knows how many actual "bad psychics" may be featured on the website, (www.badpsychics.com)? However Leslie Flint, the ultimate antithesis of a "bad psychic" and one of the greatest direct voice mediums ever, absolutely and definitely does not belong there! The only reason (if you can call it that) they put him on that site is simply because of the kind of phenomena he was involved with, no other reason! He is prejudged "guilty" by association alone and incorrectly stuffed in the same "Crackerjack box" with all the other "bad psychics" making me quite skeptical of the validity of their judgement.

The fact that Leslie Flint is on that website proves that the authors of that website consider anyone who is a psychic a bad one! Even more disturbing is how some of the individuals who posted there doubt the intelligence of anyone on the internet (calling mine and other such "woo" websites "stupid") who believes in spirits coming through seances. And if that were not bad enough, one of the regular commenters for that site would also condemn anyone with such an ability as almost criminal and always fraudulent completely regardless of who they are or what sort of phenomena they can or cannot produce when actually it is a clear indication of the commenter's bias, poor study, complete lack of appreciation, lack of knowledge and lack of interest in the extremely rare phenomenon of ectoplasm and the direct voice. This website's inclusion of Leslie Flint in the "bad psychic Crackerjack box" is a classic example of prejudicial condemnation without careful investigation.

Regarding those who are still very skeptical, it is only because they have not yet studied carefully and been able to identify the most honorable sources of this subject closely enough with an open mind, and with enough dedication and interest. They also lack personal experience of afterlife phenomena, which unfortunately is rarely or never experienced by those who are mentally and emotionally closed off to such things. Of course I do feel sorry for all those who never had any personal experiences like I have encountered, because such experiences are almost always extremely positive and provide personal proof and tremendous reassurance. The fact of its rarity unfortunately helps to keep this material world trapped in its own darkness.

Some of the most materialistic skeptics just don't want to accept that there is life after death anyway because it contradicts their personal interest and personal outlook and/or religious beliefs. Because any mediumistic phenomena would clash sharply with their life-long materialistic belief systems, no matter how obvious the evidence, nothing whatsoever will ever convince them otherwise; it would be just too far of a quantum leap for them to jump! Therefore any alleged seances with ectoplasm, trumpets whirling in mid air, disembodied voices, spirit lights, etc. are too weird and too "Hollywood" to be allowed in their concept of reality and are therefore instantly dismissed as utter nonsense!

One can put definite, indisputable, obvious proof of survival right in the face of any biased sceptic, and still the prejudiced debunker would never accept it no matter what, because it violently clashes with the skeptic's deeply engraved, all too comfortable way of thinking and living. This is unfortunate, because when such people pass over, they risk getting trapped into long periods of self-delusion, and earthbound states (clinging to Earth because materialism is all they have known and accepted) which could otherwise be avoided. However, regardless if one likes it or not, there is life after death! And for those who are humane, nonjudgmental, kindhearted, goodnatured, and know what to expect, it is extremely good!

2.4 - Leslie's "Etheric" Guests Never Coughed or Sputtered

After careful analysis of over 200 direct voice recordings, I have noticed some interesting facts. Even though Leslie Flint himself often coughed and exhibited many other cold symptoms (he seemed nearly always to sound like he had some kind of upper respiratory illness), not one of the "etheric" guests have ever coughed, cleared his or her throat, sniffed, or sneezed.

Nearly every resident of the UK in those days often had severe colds so if these "spirits" were somehow accomplices, actors, actresses, etc. how was he always able to get voices - and often the same guide, Mickey - who never coughed or sniffled? With the exception of the occasional stutterer, and some whispering voices (some spirits who had not yet mastered the etheric voice box could only whisper and breathe heavily), the souls showed no signs whatsoever of any upper respiratory aliments, lack or excess of saliva, or any other disease or unhealthy condition.

Another thing: the souls are rarely short for words, they are often immensely articulate, amazingly brilliant, and always filled to overflowing with genuine enthusiasm to communicate their message of life eternal and life after death experiences with profound love, wit, wisdom, and inspiration going on and on for up to 20 to 45 minutes at a time without stopping to take a breath.

However a rather bizarre change in pitch occurred when one lady (Jenny Wilson - recorded in 1971) went from sounding like a young lady to an old man in one session which may have been due to what she explained as drifting off a few times - causing a change in frequency. Right at the start of the recording, Jenny Wilson sounded as if she was reading from some notes, even after directly answering some questions! Probably just her way of speaking when first getting started which, like most souls speaking through the ectoplasm, is a little slow and deliberate at first and then speeding up in tempo later on in the seance as they seem to "warm up."

2.5 - Messages From the Afterlife - How the

Paranormal Voices Came Through

The direct voice mediumship of Leslie Flint is a triple miracle. It is a miracle enough that any messages from the afterlife came through at all. The second miracle is that the length, variety of personalities, and quality of communication is the greatest and highest I have ever heard in the history of mediumship. The third miracle is that other great souls such as Dr. Marshall, John Whitehead (Mickey), etc. managed to help bring through souls from rather high planes of consciousness who would not otherwise have been able to come through at all such as Rabindranath Tagore, St. Matthew, and Mahatma Gandhi. Great spiritual truths rarely heard of in seances were spoken of at great length and recorded on hours and hours of tape.

Hundreds of paranormal voice message tapes can be heard on the **Leslie Flint Educational Trust** website. Most of the communicators who come through from the other side have either British, Scottish, American, Indian or Italian accents, and some are clear and others are not. Some come through in foreign languages, and sometimes even in dead languages. The voices come from both men and women and some are from children such as Bobby Tracy (recorded Jan. 30, 1967).

Bobby Tracey was an inimitable British 5-year-old school boy who naturally communicated simple honesty yet remarkable intelligence, candid humor and an absolute uniqueness of character. He actually would have to have "died" first to come through just the way he did! If he was just an actor fraudulently mimicking a spirit, then who directed this downright fantastic sound track? Who dreamt up the "soapy bubbles" coming out of George Woods' "funny" head and why even choose such a weird subject? Who wrote the script? Who's overworked imagination was this? How did they get five-year old Bobby to sound so authentic, so natural, so impulsive, so spontaneous and so happy and carefree if it were all just a lie?

Where did all the money come from to create this effect and why even go to all the expense and trouble in the first place with just average quality recording equipment? How did they get Bobby to sound so spontaneously silly, happy and honest about having died with his mother in a fatal auto accident?

How were they able to keep Bobby's unpredictable, natural, innocent and playful spontaneity fully within the context of a remarkably realistic afterlife perspective (consistent with all the other recordings) throughout this entire 20 minute uninterrupted, unedited 1967 soundtrack? Where is this actor now? Who paid him to keep quiet when he could have made a pretty penny exposing Leslie Flint as a charlatan? Investigate this recording as much as you can! Anyone with enough common sense studying this subject carefully and close enough should have no recourse but to accept it!

It is best to use headphones and to turn down the base or adjust and process the sound through an electronic equalizer if possible. However, the subjects are so utterly interesting, it is far more than worth the trouble of listening and some are actually very clear. Many of the voices start out slow and cumbersome, speed up to a crescendo and then tend to putter out right at the very end as "the power" runs out.

Because they are communicating directly from their subtle bodies, some of the spirits do not stop for breath and start speaking unusually rapid, making themselves sound a little strange or unworldly, while others do breathe (yes spirits do breathe!) but rarely stop to think because access to their own thoughts and memories are so much clearer than when obstructed by the physical body.

The medium, Leslie Flint, usually fully conscious and conversing with both the spirits and the witnesses, provides most of the ectoplasm and energy for the spirits to create the voice box to speak through. What is ectoplasm? Ectoplasm is an extremely radiation sensitive, intermediary, vital, living, substance that coats the cells of one's spiritual body in such a way that the spirit can temporarily interact with those in the physical world. Unfortunately, any actual manifestation of ectoplasm tends to be so uncommon that most scientists conveniently dismiss it, saying there is no such thing. As if to make matters worse there are and have been plenty of hoaxes created by unscrupulous charlatans.

Leslie Flint's direct voice is a form of physical mediumship of which there are several different kinds and is, for many reasons much rarer than mental mediumship (channeling). Only a percentage of one in a million can be a physical medium and of those who are potentially gifted, very few may even realize it.

In some cases, especially during a physical manifestation or materialization seance, the spirits use an ectoplasmic larynx directly molded over and therefore resembling and instantly creating a temporary physical counterpart of the soul's vocal cords and mouth as is done in the David Thompson seances.

However, the voices through Leslie Flint used an etheric box that receives a spirit's thoughts which is somehow transmitted to an ectoplasmic larynx having the qualities drawn or "molded" from Leslie Flint and possibly from others in the group. This method saves much life force energy for more rapid, clearer communications; however they do not always closely resemble the original voices of the spirits when they were physically alive on Earth.

When using this method, a spirit has to remember how he or she sounded on Earth, while maintaining a certain level of energy, vibration and concentration on the voice box which often wavers or fluctuates. A huge book can be (and should be!) written on this subject alone being as wondrously complex as it is unbelievable.

At first it seems so amazing that they sound as natural as they do, however after closer study of this subject I now realize that it is because their world, being even more natural than ours, also has an atmosphere (or many atmospheres) and their natural (astral) bodies seem to have a beating heart and breathing lungs just as we do. People never lose all the "physical" aspects of how they were on Earth when they pass over.

Communication is a complex process requiring loving dedication and cooperation on both sides of life. Just as with any complex system, occasional "technical" difficulties with the ectoplasm do occur. Voices sometimes come through only as whispers, or the pitch may go down or up, making the person sound rather hoarse or like he or she has laryngitis.

Once in a while, two distinct voices can be heard at a time (in addition to the voices of those present with Leslie Flint often coughing) with all conversing naturally with each other. When or if two or more spirits share the same voice box, they may tend to sound exactly the same especially when or if one spirit acts as a channel (medium) for another spirit existing on a higher vibrational level.

It is a miracle enough to have any sort of communication come through at all. However, much of the information that came through regarding the descriptions of the afterlife left me absolutely spellbound. When one hears descriptions of "everyday" life in the astral worlds, one cannot help but become completely astonished at how utterly natural and ordinary are the ways of life in the finer realms beyond the veil of death.

Part 3 - Life in the Astral Worlds

3.1 - The Exciting Reality of it All

Listening to all these life after death experiences and descriptions of "the undiscovered country" is always incredible, thrilling, breathtaking, and astounding. When I first heard some of this material I could not contain my excitement, I became a raving maniac and to the annoyance of my associates, it was all I could talk about for weeks! It is so fantastic! It is so much like being in "The Twilight Zone" or in some other science fiction program, or seeing for the first time full color panoramic photos of another planet, or realizing that a miracle of biblical proportions just took place as if Moses himself just came back and divided the Red Sea again. In fact even Saint Matthew himself came back to speak in a recorded Leslie Flint seance.

Then again, I was just as dumbfounded by the almost universal lack of interest, and sometimes even complete rejection, fear and/or hatred of this subject of spiritualism. I have no doubt whatsoever of Leslie Flint's mediumship, and the only real darkness in this world comes from the darkness of those who's belief systems are too closed-minded, materialistic and restricted to know the real truth. Don't you just hate those closed-minded materialistic skeptical debunker "professors" who always seem to "officially" condemn a subject without first carefully studying it? They have to be the ultimate practitioners of "professional" mental laziness!

"Condemnation without investigation is the height of ignorance." - Albert Einstein

Apparently, even Albert Einstein hated prejudiced debunkers. Anyway, I can now confidently enjoy the excitement, awe and wonder of learning everything I can about this amazing "undiscovered country" that lies beyond all the horizons of our physical reality here on Earth. Now that I have been listening to the "Leslie Flint" voices for several months, I fully realize the sheer enormity and gravity of the need to establish communication between the worlds as easily as calling someone in a different country would have to be the greatest breakthrough in the history of humankind. This possibility is not science fiction or some fantasy.

The afterlife is as real as you and I and in many ways is even more real because of its finer nature, intelligence, texture and subtlety of consciousness. Therefore, the astral planes are not at all the dreamy, fairylike, wishy-washy worlds often populated with the spaced-out beings that are described by so many popular authors and books on the subject of the hereafter.

Those who have written about their astral travels to these planes are often limited in their descriptions because the physical and astral brains operate on a different level and so much gets lost in the translation to physical memory that the subconscious mind and dream states get in the way. I do a little astral projection myself, but tend to forget most of it! In spite of all these difficulties, astral projection can still be a reliable and wondrous way to discover what the truth is regarding the afterlife.

The reason the astral and spiritual worlds are far more natural, free, superior, alive, and comprehensive than anyone or anything on Earth is that the reality of the afterlife consists of much finer atoms, particles, energies, higher dimensions, and intelligent laws and forces than all the heavier, more massive and awkward material atoms and laws of physics physical things are made from and subject to. Life on Earth is only a pale reflection of the life to come.

Far from being the highest, the physical level is actually one of the crudest levels of existence there is. There are many much higher and finer levels of existence or vibration (spheres) to ascend into, and endless numbers of places, things to do, discover and explore, and vast amounts of information on every subject available and an expansion of awareness and knowledge that goes way beyond materialistic earthly concepts.

3.2 - An Absolutely Natural, Complete and Profoundly Fulfilling Existence

These vast, and often inconceivable worlds are filled with absolute thrills and marvels many of which, especially on the higher planes, are very hard to describe, in fact are too beautiful to describe. The planes or spheres of existence closest to Earth tend to be the easiest to describe in terms the average person can comprehend. But there are much activity and amazing civilizations on all spheres, on all levels. There are beautiful cities, towns, villages, art colonies, art galleries, movie theaters, stages, operas, museums, schools, stores (not commercial), libraries, vast natural landscapes, continents, forests, gardens, huge flowers, very tame loving animals, mountains, meadows, plains, seas, boats, ships, yachts, lakes, waterfalls, and anything and everything else really wonderful and good that one can imagine and not imagine. (God I wish I could go there, take some photos, come back and upload them to my website!)

Regarding what it is exactly like to live in even higher spheres beyond the ordinary astral worlds: imagine all the above but with an extra dimension or dimensions added, with even more colors along with even higher and deeper levels of sensitivity, sophistication, beauty, love, opportunity, and levels of consciousness with the absolute beauties of nature multiplied hundreds and hundreds of times over evolving on to infinity.

No mystic teaching or religion can or has correctly foretold the actual life after death experiences we will all one day so intensely enjoy! God knows how much I have distorted it in my own feeble attempts to describe it. Trying to explain this form of existence is even harder than trying to talk about colors with a blind person, because there are so many new levels of experience that these souls are trying to convey that simply do not exist in the limited materialistic terms and concepts that we on Earth are stuck with. Many of the souls would never want to go back to live on Earth which is in comparison to heaven, a very limited, elementary, primitive state of life indeed.

3.3 - The Colors Are Far More Vivid, Extensive and Varied

In the astral worlds the souls often marvel at all the new colors they can see! They say they can perceive and enjoy many new colors in nature that go far beyond the physical spectrum and some souls have counted as many as 77 colors. I am assuming that this phenomenon of advanced and extended color perception is due to a remarkable extension of visual sensitivity beyond violet into much higher frequencies of light such as UV, X-rays, and gamma rays and perhaps even into the lower wavelengths beyond the red spectrum as well such as infrared and microwaves, etc. but I am even less sure of this, as I would suppose perception is much more likely extended only toward the higher end of the electromagnetic spectrum rather than the lower end, as souls often say they are much more aware of higher vibrations rather than lower ones.

3.4 - Eating and Sleeping in the Afterlife

One man (Sid Hopkins) said his first experience right after dying was finding himself comfortably sitting in a parlor of a lovely, familiar place being served with a cup of tea by his wife who had died 15 years ago, yet looked like she was in her early twenties. At least two other times in the seances, a certain individual was welcomed to his new life with either a beautiful young woman or one's very lovely wife wearing a beautiful outfit serving tea!

In yet another seance it was a lovely woman serving a glass of lemonade from a freshly squeezed lemon! Yes, new arrivals to the spiritual life are often warmly welcomed with food and/or beverages by deceased relatives and/or friends looking many years younger and in a posh setting. One would often "live" on a light diet or fruit, soups and/or teas, etc. before realizing that eating and drinking is no longer really needed or necessary and is just a condition of mental habit however strong and real it may seem at first.

Instead of possibly starving or feeling hungry, one should continue to eat a little at first anyway until one no longer feels the need. Many souls even after years of astral life still on social occasions like to eat and serve light snacks, beverages and fruit. I have not yet heard of heavier foods such as meat and/or fish being served, but if they could imagine it, I suppose they would be able to enjoy that too.

The conditions of life vary considerably from sphere to sphere. The ones nearest the Earth vibration can be quite physical and according to the famous Brazilian spiritist and author of **Nosso Lar**, Francisco C. Xavier, there are conditions of living in the afterlife that are so similar to Earth, that growing and eating food (agriculture) is surprisingly common on the lowest astral planes using irrigation systems, sunlight, and fertile soils just as one would do on Earth. Only difference is, eating is not as essential, and by variance of degree, always possible to gradually evolve into a state of being no longer dependent on the habit of eating which is more of a strong psychological need than an actual physical one.

The need to rest in the afterlife can also reflect one's earthly habitual patterns, which eventually wear off too. There are periods of twilight and restfulness that souls enjoy but no actual night or darkness except in the lower spheres. Those who first enter the afterlife often go through a deep, rejuvenating sleep lasting for several days, depending on the need and development of the individual. After that deep rest, one never really sleeps again except after many, many years later in preparation to enter into yet a higher sphere at the end of their interests and activities in a lower sphere. They can and often do come back to the lower sphere(s) to teach and share spiritual truths.

3.5 - Afterlife Interests, Skills and Hobbies

Amazingly, even after one has passed away, one can continue many interests, hobbies, etc. such as gardening, reading and needlework Rose Hawkins, for example, was fairly illiterate on Earth but learned to read in the afterlife! and pursue others that one was not able to on Earth. For instance, if a frustrated musician on Earth had not much time to learn how to play a musical instrument such as a piano or guitar or a frustrated artist to paint landscapes and/or portraits, or a gardener who never had a garden on Earth, or a woodsman who would love to cut trees to make furniture, do carving, etc; well these people and those in many other fields of activity would all find excellent opportunities to fully express their talents in the astral worlds.

Spirits often say they are extremely busy with a very definite sense of deep meaning and purpose. Other skills and talents often encouraged in the astral life include teaching, singing, dancing, playwriting and acting. I am also quite sure there are all kinds of sports, games, etc. too, especially for children such as dominos enjoyed by 5-year-old Bobby Tracy. In his most funny and remarkable (full of surprises) account of the afterlife, he said his drawing ability and perspective improved quite a bit since he died.

Imagine golfing or playing croquet, football, cricket, or any other such game on an astral plane! There is also horse riding, hiking, cycling, boating and rafting etc. through beautiful natural parks. If one's more serious occupation or interest is in a creative, scientific, botanical, zoological, anthropological, historical, clerical, medical, (bio)chemical, psychological, spiritual or instructional field of endeavor, one can continue one's profession quite naturally in the afterlife and expand it to entirely new, much less materialistic levels of service.

One can still use one's own hands to create things such as clothing, curtains, decorations, musical instruments, furniture, houses, buildings, etc. from natural materials some of which are entirely different from those of Earth. Most of the souls say, except on the highest vibrational spheres, one can't just think about it and then it's there, there is a certain process to it and one must make at least some effort of some sort to create something.

However work is a joy and never tedious because one rarely feels tired, bored or inept. One can learn any new skill quickly and easily as there are far fewer physical and mental limitations like those endured on Earth. Interestingly enough, one of the spirits who came through Leslie Flint (Rose Hawkins) said that she would spend her time knitting, reading and going to town to watch movies with friends. She said she even went to get her hair cut! (Would that mean that there are astral hair salons?)

There are huge libraries filled with duplicates of every worthy and interesting book or magazine or film imaginable both written on Earth and in the astral. One spirit who never learned how to read on Earth, actually took the trouble to learn how to read in the afterlife so that she could properly enjoy all those books! Even though it is possible in the afterlife for one to get information from any book or object just by touching it, it is still advisable to know how to read and write, such subjects, along with geography, science, and history are taught in many schools throughout the afterlife.

Also there are many, many more non-materialistic subjects taught in astral schools and universities of mainly a psychic and spiritual nature. Many classes are taught by teachers and masters from higher spheres using thought forms and thought images.

3.6 - Lifestyles in the Afterlife

There may very well be certain forms of trade and/or barter in the various conditions of life, cultures, etc. found on some of the lower spheres, but I have yet to hear of anything to do with the actual existence of money, accounting systems, or banking, etc. An economic system is not at all needed on the astral planes because one's character, thoughts, karmic conditions, powerful innate creative abilities, and mental/emotional outlook seem to create and/or attract whatever is needed.

One's desires, level of intelligence, mental/emotional outlook, and heartfelt motives determine exactly what one does, experiences and gets to have in the way of companions, housing, land, personal items, and clothing (which often resembles Roman togas and/or Grecian robes, etc.) The astral worlds seem to be a dynamic mixture of completely real, natural, material, objective realities yet strongly influenced or molded by creative, positive thought forces or intentions. This is how everything natural in the way it was experienced on Earth is uniformly combined with the most perfect circumstances and joy and happiness possible. It is quite remarkable.

The spirits often say it is a perfect world and they have never, ever been happier and to never fear dying because dying is absolutely the best thing that had ever happened to them! They are quite content and are often bewildered when told that there will always be even more beautiful, even lovelier, higher places or spheres they can evolve and move into.

Part 4 - Spiritual Difficulties and Challenges

4.1 - Why Some Souls Start Out Earthbound

Search and rescue of earthbound souls is a common and very much needed occupation as many materialistic souls (not knowing anything about the astral planes or life after death) still cling to the earth for days, weeks, even months after they die simply because they know of nothing better and would often try to get the attention of their physical relatives and friends or take free rides up and down the streets on a bus!

The only real problems encountered are those souls with very strong misconceptions (such as deep religious and old, life-long dogmatic convictions) about the afterlife. They are very hard to reach and often stay earthbound much longer than most souls and usually end up in a colony on one of the "belief system territories" of the lower astral worlds along with many other souls of that same very limiting religion or belief system. They are in most cases quite happy there, so might as well leave them well enough alone!

4.2 - Is There a Hell? Are There Negative Experiences in the Afterlife?

There is neither an actual "Christian" hell or "Christian" heaven in the afterlife. If one really wants to know what hell is like, simply look around! Pardon the joke, however, it seems the physical world and all its problems, overpopulation, natural and ecological disasters, wars, crime, poverty, loneliness, stress, anxiety, mental and physical diseases, aging, etc. are more than enough to make life on Earth a really hellish place!

The idea that one would also have to face "eternal damnation" simply for not accepting or adopting someone's else's religious belief system after all the "hell" one has gone through on Earth already would be utterly unfair and utterly terrible! This concept is as bad as the atheistic belief that all one's consciousness or identity permanently ends when the heart stops.

Even though many souls at first may experience various "astral" versions of what they believe heaven or hell should be like, however there is no actual eternal hell and no actual devils toasting hapless victims on an ethereal barbecue nor spiking them with pitchforks in an eternal broiler oven! Conversely, there will never be any actual angels singing Christmas carols for eternity on harps either.

These manipulative concepts were designed to control

people's behavior, and to keep them from straying too far from their church. If the unbearable consequences of eternal damnation for not correctly following the Christian "recipe" were real, then everyone in the universe would be Christians! Belief systems that are out of alignment with one's true Self should be avoided, shredded and discarded; they simply cause far too many problems and create too many illusions. How hellish or heavenly life will be both here and hereafter depends entirely on one's "thought matrix" or habitual levels of thinking and feeling. The relationship of one's state of being to one's experiences in life is a perfect equation.

There are many hellish states of consciousness possible in the afterlife with the corresponding realms or vistas of creation that resemble these states. Hell is really a state of mind which one is more likely to experience in the physical realm than in the realm of spirit, which is usually far too subtle to allow it. One of the first things everyone experiences after dying is God's unconditional love and profound, all-embracing, all-healing Light of deep wisdom and knowledge. This wonderful Light comes from the vibration of multidimensional space at a quantum level and is responsible for the creation and expansion of the universe.

Many Christians are most likely to experience this

intelligent, warm, compassionate Light as Jesus or Mary. They will discover that "God" or "Jesus" or "Mary" has a wonderful sense of humor and will thoughtfully answer all questions. This light is actually one's Higher Self of all humanity and will lovingly reveal its Self in whatever religious figure, form or symbol one ascribes to God(dess). This Self is the same Self that dwelled in the body of Jesus and countless other most beloved avatars and masters throughout the ages.

However, those who have been thoughtless and uncaring, full of hatred and malice toward others, downright evil or completely materialistic, had no sense of love of compassion for others, had no inclinations toward spirituality, or had very strong but incorrect religious convictions, will encounter some complications in the afterlife. The ones who treated others badly will have to experience all the negative things done to others in a rather extensive and panoramic life review before being allowed to go further.

Thieves and murderers will find themselves in dark, desolate communities filled with other thieves and murderers, or be completely alone or isolated for eons, or will haunt the world as an earthbound spirit continuing to influence others in very negative ways and therefore creating even more pain for themselves to face when they finally get round to encountering the Light again.

In reality there is only one quantum consciousness shared by all life forms, and one will have to experience everything they did to all other life forms. Simple physics even applies to the soul: "**What you put out is what you get back.**" Simply follow the Golden Rule: "**Do unto others as you would have others do unto you.**"

There is no escaping one's soul which really is the harshest judge of all, because nothing in every moment of one's life is left uncovered. Many souls such as Hitler or Stalin (and possibly Osama bin Laden after being killed in 2011) most likely suffered huge regrets after passing over and realizing how badly they screwed up. Because there ultimately is only one supreme Soul, the Light of Spirit must reveal to them all of the consequences of their sadly misguided intentions upon awakening into this Light, forcing them to experience of all the misery and suffering they caused others. Many such individuals would tend to live in the dark realms for hundreds, if not thousands of years to hide from the Light of their higher Self until they can face up to the consequences of their mistakes.

4.3 - What Happens When One Abuses Power?

Oppression of others is stupid behavior because there is

only one Self, one Universal Consciousness shared by countless individuals. The consequences of everyone's actions never go away, because what one does to others is actually done to one's greater Self.

I am often appalled at all the crime and other abusive behavior one can see in the news every day. This world, this earth seems so often to be turned on its head by those in power who should otherwise be serving the common good, serving humanity with great efficiency rather than exploiting humanity for his or her own selfish motives.

One of the single most common, most appalling, and most tragic and stupid mistakes throughout the history of humankind, is to yield to the temptation of gaining power only to abuse it, and only to take advantage of and to oppress others. This stupid behavior causes overall inefficiency in human progress toward complete freedom from all suffering, wars, crime, shortages, inequality and ignorance. In other words, the world could have been an infinitely better place if only certain individuals in power would just relinquish the stupid tendencies of dominance, lust for control, and repression of others.

Any soul who would misuse one of the rarest opportunities ever to faithfully serve humanity on a vast scale will sorrowfully regret his or her abuse of that power for nearly an eternity. Whenever life's circumstances gives a person a truly great once-in-a-thousand-lifetimes' opportunity to change the world for the better on a massive level, only for that person to yield to the temptations of materialism, lust, power, greed, egotism, conspiracies, oppression, etc.; this person has committed the worse sin ever, because this person has willfully hurt massive numbers of good, peace-loving people. Similarly, one person can only do so much harm or good with a bicycle, while those with a stealth fighter can do far more extreme harm or good and will, of course reap whatever they sow.

The materialistic atheist has no concept of the Self, that eternal Self that can never be escaped from. One way or another he or she has to pay dearly for every evil deed done to another. The dark, evil materialist after the time of death must either remain earthbound and/or must go (sometimes right away, sometimes eventually) to a truly horrible, dark, cold and morbid realm of one's own making to be trapped there until one fully realizes the terrible wrongs this person has committed. Only through sincere regret can there ever be any hope of redemption.

Fortunately, there is no such thing as an eternal hell nor any sort of permanent punishment. However one, can be mired in some of the most unpleasant consequences of one's actions for a very long time. As previously mentioned, the eternal fire and damnation of Christian theology remains only as a creation of one's belief system which must dissolve in the light of truth. The actual hells that do exist are the cold, dark, bare granite rock dimensions of reality that exist on levels of vibration beneath the earth vibration. The more evil and deprived one is, the more limited one will be to within these dimensions.

The Rev. Howard Storm was originally an atheist with a rather bad temperament and living a life of selfish materialism. During a truly life-transforming and rather shocking near-death experience, he was forced by a group of "evil" souls to one of these dark realms and torn to shreds by them, yet survived and came back to Earth to talk about it! He is now a Christian minister dedicating his life to the service and love of humanity. Having experienced what a hellish afterlife is like and having also been shown the immense good he could now do, become, and experience, he came back to Earth turned around 180 degrees opposite of the negative person he was before his incredible experience!

One can go ahead and deny all the overwhelming evidence there is for life after death and its very profound implications and consequences, but it is as factual as any other truth. Not just the existence of heavenly realms, but also the existence of countless dark and morbid realms for those whose minds and hearts are violently opposed to unconditional love, spirit, reverence for life and compassion for others, have been confirmed by countless mediums, yogis, and near-death experiencers throughout history.

God never intended to create a hellish afterlife. These dark and terrible realms nearest to the Earth vibration would otherwise be just peaceful places of rest and transition to the glorious realms of astral and spiritual heaven. It is the criminal souls who find themselves stuck in that realm who, by the law of attraction (which operates much faster in the afterlife realms) have turned it into a hell or cosmic prison of their own making. Man, through the law of cause and effect by his own evil actions and thoughts, created various types or levels of hell in what otherwise would have been a calm, serene, blank or neutral background of restful darkness.

Only the lower spheres (of what otherwise would have been peaceful) can accomodate such levels of deprived cruelty and cruddy expressions of those steeped in greed, materialism, abuse of others, ignorance, selfishness, and nonchalant egotism. The earth is unfortunately surrounded by a thick, dark, cold ethereal fog of fear and confusion caused by all the world's negative thoughts, egotistic materialism, greed, separatism, and ignorant selfishness.

There is always hope, however, for the wayward materialistic and selfish soul who through the consequences of his dark thoughts, intentions and actions, finds himself stuck in a terrible afterlife. The first thing such a dark soul should do is to realize how stupidly selfish (evil) his decisions have been and then call for help. Plenty of help for sincere souls anywhere in the universe is always available by spirit guides from the upper realms!

Once counseled and sorted out and in order to enter into the realms of the "Light," the wayward soul must undergo a life review (which happens automatically whenever one turns toward the "Light" for the first time) where every emotional pain inflicted on others has to be experienced. Then this soul knows for sure exactly how terrible a monster he or she was on Earth and begs for a way to remonstrate. He or she is then given several choices by spirit guides on how to do so. Often such a being will feel a tremendous desire to return to Earth to try to correct and/or pay for all wrongs previously committed.

The wayward soul is sometimes guided to a kind of hospital or half-way house on one of the mid or lower astral planes and given certain choices: whether to return to Earth to pay off the karmic debts owed through suffering and service to others on Earth, or stay in the astral realms to learn how to help others in similar situations as this wayward soul had been in and then possibly reincarnate later.

Once one is utterly humbled by a rotten life on Earth and/or sick and tired of the limitations of physical existence and paid off vast amounts of karmic debt through stoically taking other people's abuse and service to others, the soul need not ever return (reincarnate) and is free to go on into the higher realms where true, everlasting fulfillment can be found.

Important note regarding reincarnation: because of the vast, multidimensional nature of the soul, God and reality, reincarnation may not simply be the returning of one soul to Earth as a new-born but as an oversoul with multiple or simultaneous incarnations.

4.4 - The Problem with Suicide

This subject is one of the most touchy and sensitive issues I've ever written about. I sincerely apologize to anyone offended by what I am about to say. All situations are different and quite individual, therefore please keep in mind that any consequences of completing a suicide entirely depend on the circumstances leading up to the incident and that none of my statements can ever apply to all cases.

With the above statement aside, after knowing just how wonderful death really is, why don't we all just kill ourselves and go back to paradise? One would think, especially if one is in a terrible predicament or suffering or pain or some other severe hardship that one might as well take one's own life and get it over with. After all, so many of the souls who come through can't help but say how extremely happy they are to be free from all the miseries and complexities of physical living and that death was the best thing that ever happened to them. However, the spirits warn that to go before one's time would be detrimental to spiritual wholeness.

Would suicide ever be justified? An assisted suicide might make sense for those patients who are on the life support, in intensive care, who are being forced to hang around in a "vegetable" state of total or extreme disability and/or who are only suffering and having no chance whatsoever of any future purpose, convalescence, joy, healing or happiness while still on Earth. If the physical body is very old, completely worn out, completely useless, in a coma, etc. then why on Earth prolong the suffering? Why not allow the soul its freedom of choice so that it can go on if it wants to? To deliberately force the soul to stay stuck in a painful, agonizing existence in a completely worn-out body and non-functioning brain would not make any sense whatsoever.

On the other hand, if one is still young, healthy, and can still in any way shape or form do some sort of good or service to humanity while still on Earth, it could be a digression to one's spiritual progress or development to complete suicide, which would rather be like quitting school before one graduates or cutting "Earth" classes before the course is over. There is no such thing as a "shortcut" to paradise. To enter paradise, one's self-concept must be very upright or full of certainty or knowing that one has done only the best thing possible while on Earth with whatever hardship or seeming injustices thrown at one and has not overindulged in too much selfish behavior to the detriment of others. One must face one's self and that is the catch. Whatever one does, one must "live" with all the consequences of that decision, and experience the thoughts and emotions of all the people hurt by or affected in any way by the taking of one's own life.

Regarding life on Earth, no matter how difficult, suicide is obviously a most unpleasant option, and death is not intended or designed to solve all one's problems, which are trying to teach one some very important lessons, not to mention all the very important reasons for being on Earth in the first place. Will some souls who completed suicide while stil in the prime of life lament at the grief and sadness they may have caused others to go through, lost opportunities to love, grow, experience and really become the person they always wanted to be? Yes there is always that risk, but nearly all suicides are due to deep depression or desperately trying to avoid a terrible circumstance.

Every incarnated soul has a mission of some sort to accomplish, and from what I've learned, heard and read about suicide, to find one's self back "at home" without having first accomplished all that one has intended to do on Earth could sometimes result in having to gather more experiences from Earth. Life, whether here or hereafter is a responsibility. Could that responsibility ever be escaped from without sacrifice to one's spiritual evolution and progress toward finer levels of happiness, fulfillment and salvation?

4.5 - The Problem With Reincarnation (Not My Favorite Subject)

Very few souls ever want to go back to live (reincarnate) on Earth again. Some souls say reincarnation is possible, and there are many proven cases of reincarnation. According to a video of Betty Jean Eadie, author of **Embraced by the Light** there might be a form of reincarnation but nothing like what common eastern and popular western "New Age" concepts portray. According to the medium Robert James Lees (1849-1931), author of **The Life Elysian**, his spirit author (or ghost writer--ha! ha!), Aphraar states that the concept that one dies and reincarnates again and again is a distortion, in other words, there is usually no personal spirit that enters the body after its conception. He also states that there are many mislead souls both on Earth and in the hereafter who will say that reincarnation is essential for spiritual and evolutionary progress, just as there are many who pass over still believing in old religious philosophies or dogmas, because no one suddenly becomes all-knowing wise and perfect just because they died.

William Charles Cadwell who is direct voice medium David Thompson's main spirit convener at the **Circle of the Silver Cord**, stated in one of the seances that half of the souls born onto the "Earth plane" have lived at least once before, while the other half are new souls with no past except as pure "quantum" energy. Getting exact, scientific knowledge of reincarnation even while in direct communication with spirits is still quite a challenge.

Even though knowledge in the afterlife is so much easier to obtain and retain, the spirits can still carry with them many misconceptions and contradictions just as they had while on Earth. Other than for a great soul to come back as a teacher (like Yogananda or Jesus Christ), I would have to seriously question the reasoning of anyone who would want to come back and live on Earth again! My official view on reincarnation: it not only is possible, it is constantly occurring and is, unfortunately, essential for all souls who are still tied up with the Earth vibration. However, I personally dislike the idea of becoming physically restricted again after any period of heavenly freedom!

Anyway, I am still wondering about the sanity of those few souls on the other side who say they want to reincarnate! For example there is a tape recording where Annie Besant, a famous Theosophist talks for a while about reincarnation and spiritual development followed by an Italian lady named Estell (near end of tape) who wants to reincarnate so she could get married and have children which was not possible for her during her recent lifetime on Earth. (Why can't she do this on the astral plane where everyone's desire is provided for?) Annie Besant, who believed she herself would reincarnate right away (but speaking through Leslie Flint's ectoplasm 55 years after her death obviously did not!) states that there are group souls who reincarnate together to express truth and to uplift humanity. However I am a little uncomfortable and worried about what she says about reincarnation as if the time spent on Earth was so insignificant which may be true from the cosmic perspective, but from my viewpoint, just my present lifetime on Earth alone has been a rather traumatic, tiresome, unpleasant experience.

My concern with reincarnation is why do we souls seem to be such gluttons for punishment supposedly having had so many past lives many of which were quite tragic and then not even remembered by the vast majority? To willingly get reborn into a new body and forgetting everything previously learned to me is simply awful! Living lives on Earth compared to living lives in the heavenly spheres is usually much harder, often terrifying, and extremely frustrating!

At least it has been for me in both this lifetime in England and the U.S. and in previous lifetimes in Turkey and other parts of the Middle East where I was kidnapped, buried alive for several years, and then murdered while trying to escape, and in another life, I died by crashing through the top of a catacomb or abandoned well while riding a camel (along with several others in a caravan) over a desert hill which gave me nightmares for years while young and seemed to lead to severe problems in my present lifetime.

I also remember a vivid nightmare where I was astonished to see a prehistoric man in very primitive clothing running across a barren, rocky plain so fast right in front of my range of vision that it made me laugh until the next thing I knew my head was being crushed within the mouth of a sabertooth tiger! Glad I woke up right away!

I would never, ever want to reincarnate ever again! I mean to go through all that forgetting who we really are, birthing trauma, diapers, growing up, learning how to communicate, making the same mistakes over and over, working hard for almost nothing, choking on physical food, hunger, searching for a mate, loneliness, uncertainty, suffering, disease, and dying etc. over and over again-- who in their right mind would want to reincarnate?! It's a wonder I didn't crawl back inside whenever I was born!

The frustrating and humiliating limitations and sufferings of physical living is this main concern that has driven me nearly insane and then to yoga, meditation and afterlife research in the first place--I really need to know for sure that I won't have to leave paradise and forget my true self again through another rudely disrupting reincarnation! This is the problem of reincarnation I have been concerned about and that has prompted much of my spiritual research in the hopes of finding a way out of this rather frightening cycle of birth, suffering and death.

Another serious problem regarding reincarnation one would have to acknowledge is the fact that with the ever growing population of the earth there could never be enough reincarnating human souls to occupy all those new bodies unless perhaps they come from either nature spirits (elemental thought forces or creations), fragments of one's Oversoul and/or animal spirits, Source Energy (as Abraham-Hicks would say) or simply nothing at all except some self-aware fragment of the Universal Spirit, Prana or Shakti. The recent massive surge to nearly seven billion people proves that there can't possibly be enough reincarnations from past human lives from past history to go around unless they came from some other source or even no source at all.

According to Robert A. Monroe's **Ultimate Journey** it is the numerous separate fragments of an Oversoul who reincarnate and never one soul reincarnating over and over. When tuning in through meditation or through dream states, these past lives of those fragments of one's Oversoul could easily be experienced or interpreted as one's own. These fragments often exist as members of like-minded individuals living together in a group or community in the afterlife. I like that explanation and prefer to stick with it rather than feel I must go on and on reincarnating! This explanation is quite realistic because Robert actually met his other "soul fragments" quite frequently throughout his out-of-body adventures who were often in all sorts of states, stages and lifetimes. So have I experienced similar encounters in my dream states including fragmentary experiences of simultaneous lives in different planets, places and times as portrayed in Jane Robert's **The Oversoul 7 Trilogy**.

To even further clarify this issue, an excellent account was written that discusses how a three-year-old boy suffered from nightmares of his previous existence as a Corsair aircraft pilot assigned to the Natoma Bay in which he was shot down by the Japanese and crashed. The rest of the article discusses how when a soul reincarnates, only an aspect of itself or a facet of itself reincarnates, never the whole (group) soul at once.

Therefore, according to Silver Birch, who communicated through the trance medium Maurice Barbanell during the mid twentieth century, when one reincarnates, the original person always stays behind in spirit, while actually it is another fragment of the same oversoul of the original person who starts out in a new physical body equipped with the memories and tendencies of the original reincarnation. However, the original spirit entity may act as a spirit guide, guardian angel, feel responsible for, or closely associated with the newly incarnated soul fragment.

From these tapes, it is now confirmed that souls on the lowest level of development either come back to reincarnate right away after passing over or remain in either an unconscious (sleep) state, or are earthbound (shadow being), or remain stuck in an inferior low astral vibration or state. However, most souls, and those who are more spiritually advanced live more consciously, much more pleasantly and much longer on the astral spheres before returning to Earth again.

The great Christ-like yogi, Sri Yukteswar said in Chapter 43 "The Resurrection of Sri Yukteswar" of **Autobiography of a Yogi** by Paramhansa Yogananda that the average soul, after some 150 to 600 years of astral living must either move on to higher planes (spheres) of consciousness beyond the astral plane (the causal and celestial planes or spheres which are said to be the real heavens) or if not evolved enough to remain conscious in such a refined state of being, must return back to Earth or some other sphere, and repeat this cycle until the soul is in fact advanced enough to consciously exist on the causal plane after which point it will simply manifest back and forth between the causal and astral spheres until it remains permanently on the causal and finally celestial levels of consciousness as a "freed soul.'

Here again is more confirmation of why it is so essential to dedicate one's life to the search for truth, meditate on Spirit for long hours, evolve spiritually, become as selfless as possible, and free one's self from all material (earthly) desires and attachments forever. From all of the most authoritative material that I have read and listened to so far, most of us will have to come back again and again to reincarnate more lifetimes on Earth! Even Jesus (according to Dr. Marshall as "Lucillius") will reincarnate eventually but only as an advanced "helper" of humanity or "freed soul" or "avatar" as described in **Autobiography of a Yogi** by Paramhansa Yogananda.

An alternative to reincarnation on Earth is the possibility of reincarnation on a much "easier" sphere such as Bashar's world, Essassani mentioned later on in this article. A very physical reincarnation can be experienced on that planet, except it is still subtle enough to not be such a traumatic limitation to the soul nor have to force one to go through any other sort of unpleasantness so often typical of life's struggles on Earth.

Interesting to see in many instances how the system of

yogic knowledge and experienced astral travelers confirm all that has come through Leslie Flint and how all the more important it is to evolve spiritually or remain stuck in the quandary of spiritual ignorance and suffering of reincarnation!

The spirits say that salvation should come naturally, and to never expect it to come from some other god, guru, or person, but only through the direct experience of their teachings, and through one's own inner growth, meditation and evolution of the soul. Just as one can never reach the horizon, absolute perfection can never be reached, only approached. One can never actually become God, one can and does however get ever closer and closer to becoming like God (perfect love, freedom, spiritual light, joy and wholeness).

The physical reality is really only a very tiny, rather backwards and insignificant part of the "rainbow universe." In the higher levels of the vibrational spheres or universal spectrum of existence, most souls seem to enjoy centuries and centuries of very idealistic living while gradually evolving into ever higher and higher spheres and expanding into ever new dimensions of great love, understanding, experience, creativity and beauty indefinitely.

Part 5 - The Nature of the Astral Worlds

5.1 - Climates and Geography of the Astral Spheres

There is also air, wind and on some spheres (the spirits say there are thousands of astral worlds or spheres) occasional light rain, dew, mist, and even a light snow in the upper elevations just as happens on Earth. The weather patterns of the astral worlds tend to be mild and never contrary to the needs of the inhabitants.

The temperature ranges from mildly cool to comfortably warm depending on the original climate and conditions the inhabitants were most used to on Earth. There are all the same climates and natural conditions of life as found on Earth including deserts, mountain regions, polar regions, forest regions, tropical areas, ocean environments, and land masses ranging from vast continents to beautiful tropical islands.

Many of Leslie Flint's communicators say they have seen rivers, and lakes with some being quite vast and always quite placid and beautiful in a constantly warm summery afternoon environment. It is possible to go swimming and many souls do. One can also travel by boat or ship, and go diving, etc. One can also drink these pure waters as there is no pollution, bugs or bacteria in the ponds, lakes and rivers to worry about, and no water, air or noise pollution either as there is no need for cars, freeways, sewers and factories. The water is crystalline pure and very desirable to drink. Strangely enough, the souls often say that they can enjoy all the benefits of swimming, bathing, etc. yet are completely dry (even their clothes) the instant they get out!

Imagine an ordinary physical world of three dimensions of space and a fourth of time. Then add a fifth dimension (an extra direction for time and space to expand into) to this picture and then you have a rough idea of what the environment is like in the afterlife. While traveling up through the vibrational spheres (actually takes some practice and experience to do this), the whole landscape can transform into an astonishing variety of geographies, for example, above the location where a vast plain existed, now there's an alpine forest landscape and running fountains.

Before ascending, it was misty, now it is cloudless, and billions of subtle colors from the extended atmosphere even further above would be prismatically refracted throughout the whole glorious sky. The astral atmosphere, being much vaster than the Earth's atmosphere, would appear far deeper and, if there are clouds, would tend to have many more cloud layers.

Regarding the surface of the astral worlds: imagine countless interacting, interconnecting layers of an onion: some below the earth's surface and many above with each one having a higher and higher rate of vibration and lighter composition than the ones beneath. This rough idea would constitute the spheres of the afterlife existence one encounters. If one could visualize a four-dimensional "earth" this would be very close to actuality.

Such a four-dimensional sphere would have to have a three-dimensional "surface" that expands in size as one goes higher and higher up the scale of atomic vibration. Most matter in the universe is in fact composed of these finer substances which astronomers throughout the world can see gravitational evidence of in various parts of the distant universe. Astronomers and cosmologists are still trying to understand what "dark matter" really is. I think dark matter consists of the densest form or lowest level of astral matter vibrating at a frequencies just beyond our physical level of vibration yet still able to have a generalized or overall gravitational influence on the stars in every galaxy of the physical universe.

5.2 - The Beauty of Astral Nature and Spiritual Utopia

Some trees grow very high and can often be in full bloom and/or produce much fruit. Flowers of all kinds, shapes and sizes exist in the astral worlds and grow in moist soils just like they do on Earth. Because they are living things and very much alive, they are not to be picked and can often grow taller than houses. In fact there are whole forests of very tall flowers growing as tall as trees creating magnificent perfumes that are wafted for miles and miles on mild astral breezes.

Gardens and gardening is a very common thing among most of the souls, as most souls who have houses have and enjoy wonderful, lush gardens. Yes, nature is a very real, abundant and natural part of the astral worlds, especially the highest worlds where the beauty of nature becomes almost infinite. In fact the astral worlds may be the actual origin of all natural existence, whereas the Earth is just a dim, almost artificial reflection of what nature intends to create and manifest. To think that the physical universe is the only universe is very chauvinistic. Not only are there other existences, but far superior ones as well!

The astral planes are teeming with all sorts of both extinct and presently living plants and animals from Earth. There are no pesky insects, pests or predators whatsoever. (It is possible, however that they do exist on some of the lowest planes or spheres.) The lion definitely sleeps with the lambs and all races, creeds and nationalities definitely live in perfect harmony and peace with one another just as portrayed in those "Jehovah's Witness" illustrations in their international magazines, **Awake!** and **Watchtower**.

The funny thing is just how similar the ideal world that the Jehovah's Witness describe is to the actual descriptions by spirits. There are wonderful places or "belief system territories" in the astral worlds where even the "dead" "Jehovah's Witnesses" can hang out still waiting for that ideal new Earth to come even though there is a perfectly beautiful world right in front of their noses completely surrounding them!

5.3 - Communication With Animals and Singing in an Etheric Atmosphere

Spirits often say that if they tuned into it, there seems to be a soft, soothing, healing vibration or music in the atmosphere generated either by nature and/or creative souls who somehow recorded (left) their songs in the either. One can talk, sing, play instruments, and create sound just like on Earth, yet one can also communicate by thought and most souls quickly find that telepathy is the most efficient way to communicate especially if the other person speaks only Spanish, for instance and you only can speak English. Astonishing as this may sound, telepathic communication between animals and humans is quite easy and common on the astral levels. One spirit came through saying he had an amazing "conversation" with his deceased canine pet. There was once a David Thompson seance held at Mansfield 10th October 2007 where a barking dog materializes!

Another amazing thing is that people who have never learned to read or write properly on Earth often do in the afterlife! There are so many libraries, colleges, schools, etc. on the astral planes to learn such things as well as many other subjects ranging from basic to far beyond the scope and imagination of materiality. Joy, inspiration, breathing and laughter always comes naturally and easily; one always feels light, full or energy, vitality, and one never grows old, ill or suffer from any pains. Breathing the air is a joy, "it is just like wine" says Mary Ivan (near top of list on left) toward the end of her seance. Often the air is filled with perfumes from countless flowers naturally growing in surrounding gardens, fields, etc.

5.4 - Astral Relationships, Sex, Reproduction, Families, and Astral "Old Age"

Who has not longed to fall in love with one's soul mate, enjoying the companionship of one's true sweetheart on the highest and meaningful levels of beauty, love and fulfillment? Who has not longed for real affection, and even a fulfillment in sensuality beyond one's wildest dreams?

All of the most enjoyable aspects of marriages, relationships, etc. do not need to end at death and can go on as long as both people in the afterlife feel the need and even expand into all kinds of exciting new possibilities of love and beauty that one has always longed for but was unable to achieve on Earth. New relationships are formed all the time in the astral worlds between two souls who for some reason were unable to find love or live with each other on Earth.

However, the souls say they do not give or take in marriage as there seems to be no actual need for official marriages to take place in the afterlife because one is either together with someone or not, and therefore there is no need for contracts on paper, etc. even though that is possible and does happen!

Sex of course, still exists too on certain planes closest to the Earth's vibration. I would have to say that from many books I have read on astral projection, the spirit is indeed naturally filled with sheer vitality and youthfulness! In the initial stges of spirit life, it must be very intense and rather frequent for as long as the habit remains imprinted in the samskaras of the psyche. Just as it does on Earth, sex does seem to drain one's spirit of vitality, sense of balance and wisdom and the soul instinctively learns to either moderate, transmute, or let go of that activity for higher and even more profoundly satisfying pleasures or higher spheres of experience, knowledge and deeper, more fulfilling loves.

Otherwise, those whose attachments are still rooted in the material, may feel very much drawn back to Earth and amazingly, develop a strong desire to reincarnate long before anyone else normally would! It has been discovered that if a man from Earth tries to have sex while astral projecting, he often finds himself immediately back in his physical body. On the other hand, an astral projecting woman can more often stay in the astral during astral sex but will have more trouble later on trying to return to the astral world. What does this tendency imply for discarnate souls who have no physical body to come back to?

On the higher planes, other interests seem to take over or easily transmute sexual energy into finer and more meaningful expressions and experiences of true affection, boundless bliss, inspiration, love and ecstasy. Normally, especially while away from the influences of Earth, sex no longer seems to be an issue or a great concern anymore because of the intense joy, love, interests, profound beauties, and natural ecstasies always present in the afterlife. It may be that souls in the afterlife are often in a constant (balanced) state of joy, love and orgasm anyway, especially on the higher planes, so why would one crave or need sex if one is already so naturally fulfilled in every way, so full of peace, so full of so many different interests and curiosities, and so full of love anyway?

There are many, many dimensions to the soul that can open up and develop into phenomenal states of being. Therefore, falling in love with someone on the astral plane can become quite profound, and so awesome, it would make the simple sexual relationships enjoyed back on Earth look ridiculously shallow, limited and superficial in comparison.

One can experience an intense love and losing of the self into a greater Self, an absolutely fulfilling happiness that one can't even begin to describe. Amazingly, one need not even have to depend on a partner for this experience, and still experience this intense love for all humanity and as a result gradually transcend into ever higher and higher spheres of almost infinite beauty and love.

As bizarre and surprising as this information may sound, it is actually just as possible to create or have children on some of the most "physical" worlds of the afterlife in the exact same way it occurs on Earth because these worlds have only a slightly higher vibration rate than Earth. Like Earth, these planets have atmospheres often rich in oxygen (which the souls actually breathe!) and are directly illuminated by the stars they orbit around, and not always by the more ethereal reflected light often enjoyed by souls on the mid to high astral planets or planes.

Anything and every experience possible can be found and enjoyed in the afterlife. Only on Earth and a very few other similar places in the universe as ignorant and backwards as the Earth is there such physical limitation, confusion, suffering and darkness.

I know that nature would not have as strong a need for reproduction (replacement of bodies) in the afterlife as it does on the more rough places like Earth because of the longevity (many, many centuries before becoming "causal") of its inhabitants and the extremely benign and beautiful environments that the souls enjoy so much.

On some of the more "physical" spheres or planets in the astral universe, rebirth into their world through an "astral" pregnancy is possible. It is true that many souls can and do reincarnate on certain semi-astral or semi-physical planets like we do on Earth, except the conditions are usually not nearly as limiting, harsh or severe. Under favorable conditions and because of the excellent genetics of these beings, the life spans are often much, much longer also, sometimes extending into thousands of years.

According to Bashar (a member of an ethereal alien hybrid race channeled through the mental medium Darryl Anka) there is an ethereal yet very Earth-like planet filled with lakes, rivers, wildlife, jungles and forests called **Essassani** (Place of Living Light) some 500 light years away toward the Orion constellation that actually contains a human/grey hybrid race (the Sassani) where they still have children through birth, yet spirits can and do "pop in" from the higher realms to visit! Towards the end of one of his videos, Bashar discusses these very things.

It is this "semi-physical" mixture of matter and spirit that makes this location and race of beings a very interesting subject to study indeed! Their "quasi-physical" black triangular space craft have often been seen in many places throughout the Earth today. According to an illustration of what might be one of their ships and an article on one of the sightings by the award winning journalist, Linda Moulton Howe, on her extraordinary Earthfiles.com website, it appeared semi-transparent indicating a possible "vibrational" difference in the same way and for the same reason a ghost would appear translucent.

A soul who reincarnates on an astral planet may be one of countless causal beings still with some astral karma returning from the highly refined mental or causal spheres. This soul is reborn as a perfectly beautiful astral baby boy or girl. According to the great Christ-like yogi, Sri Yukteswar in Chapter 43, "The Resurrection of Sri Yukteswar," of **Autobiography of a Yogi** by Paramhansa Yogananda, souls returning from many centuries of bliss in the causal spheres (beyond the highest astral spheres) are actually "reborn" in new astral bodies.

The astral or "natural" body, even though outwardly the same as the physical body once was in youth, eventually through eons of time loses its internal organs one-by-one until even the physical outward appearance starts to change into a sexless being of light or becomes "causal" or no longer with an external astral body. This may in fact be what a true angel is: a being of light, so advanced that no outward astral form remains, just a structure of light in a state of profound wholeness.

Also there have always been many spirit babies and young children who passed over in early infancy, stillborn, etc. from Earth who are in need of a mother to take care of them on the the other side of death. Therefore (and this fact I know is absolutely true) those who longed to be a mother on Earth but never had the chance can find plenty of opportunity for motherhood in the astral worlds! Another great wonder is the fact that spirit infants and children can and do indeed grow up in the afterlife just as they would on Earth!

For example, Alf Pritchette, a spirit communicator on one of the seance recordings, said he was greeted by his absolutely beautiful young sister who looked nineteen or twenty and blessed with long, flowing blond hair. What is so amazing is that Alf was completely taken by surprise when he discovered he had a sister in the afterlife, let alone being all grown up and so astonishingly beautiful, because she had died in infancy and hardly remembered this even happened because it was so long ago!

This beautiful soul must have been looked after for many years by a spirit relative or relatives or other personal guardian until she had fully grown up in the astral world, most likely having gone to "astral" school and then "astral" college, etc. similar to the way she would have on Earth but without all the limitations of Earth, and lived in a beautiful country cottage and is now available to look after Alf Pritchette!

Because of the many accidents, illnesses, old age, and

other hostile conditions prevalent on Earth, sex tends to be only a very physical, down-to-earth and biological reproductive need where the replacement of bodies is essential. Unfortunately physical attraction, backgrounds, and economics are historically the main forces that create marriages on Earth.

However, love in the afterlife becomes a much more individual, meaningful, universal, satisfying and permanent expression between two souls who are usually from the same soul group. Love and affection becomes most important, while sexual attraction tends to be drowned out by intense love, affection and spiritual bliss. As a result of this tendency, relationships in the various aspects of heaven or the afterlife can be many times more harmonious and deeply meaningful.

Love and spirituality seem to come to the foreground while sex and materiality fall into the background, whereas on Earth, unfortunately it tends to be the other way around with the additional burdens of materialistic necessities such as housing, food, work, raising kids, etc. Entire families do exist on the astral planes, of course, but with only the positive, much more expansive, rewarding aspects of family love and community living.

However, it is still possible to have arguments and

clashes with one another and they do happen from time to time, as life on the astral spheres is just as natural and real, if not more so than on Earth. Therefore people who find they cannot live together in harmony simply don't and go to their separate parts of the astral spheres!

As far as the "giving and taking of marriage" is concerned, much of what was essential on Earth is no longer essential in the astral spheres. Souls freed from Earth can grow and develop in many new ways not possible or imagined while on Earth and often discover that their real soul mates (relationships based on real or spiritual love) were not the ones they had married just for economic or sexual reasons while on Earth.

In the afterlife, one is naturally linked up with the person or persons they want to be close to regardless of previous Earth marriages, relationships, etc. and such "soul mates" are usually members of one's personal soul group which is a group of souls (often hundreds of people) all sharing the same oversoul often living together in the same community at the same level or strata of consciousness. Those who had married someone who they truly loved while on Earth, will most likely be a member of the same soul group and continue that marriage into the "eternities" of the astral spheres and maybe even the finer spheres beyond the astral depending on how deep and real that love really is.

A rare and quite remarkable Leslie Flint recording (Chopin, 05.03.54) of knowledgeable spirit communicator, the famous American showman, Florenz Ziegfeld, entered the conversation with an American accent (immediately followed by another person with a Scottish accent while changing in mid sentence) presented awesome information regarding the life cycles of the astral spheres and gradual "physical" changes that occur in the human astral body over centuries of time, and fascinating information backing up what I have written so far regarding sex and reproduction in the afterlife.

According to this most amazing recording, over centuries of time, as the astral body "ages" resulting in gradual changes in the personality and emotions move toward wholeness, perfection, spiritual and cosmic inclinations. The soul eventually over eons of time gains a more unisexual appearance as tremendous love completely replaces the lower appetites such as sex.

The more physical aspects of life gradually cease to exist after successive "graduations" into ever higher and higher spheres of life. The astral body ultimately gives way to a much finer sexless "causal" body of light and according to Sri Yukteswar in Chapter 43 "The Resurrection of Sri

Yukteswar" in **Autobiography of a Yogi** by Paramhansa Yogananda, the soul after the astral body completely drops off, according to its inclination, level of development, etc., either must immediately return to Earth or hopefully go on to the causal spheres to be later reborn over and over as an astral being until it no longer even needs to be reborn as an astral person.

The sheer complexity, subtleties and vastness of all the cycles and dimensions of life in the afterlife is impossible to fully depict or explain in ordinary terms. One lifetime on Earth is really just a microscopic sliver in the vast ocean of all the other lives and aspects of experience that awaits every single soul beyond the veil of death. Earth too is really just another "astral" planet except with an unusual degree of density where most beings struggling to live there are strongly bound to the limiting laws of physicality. The same limitations apply to any "astral" planet anywhere in the universe at the same physical level as Earth's.

5.5 - Illumination (Sun?) of the Astral World

The sun still shines or at least seems to emanate some kind of effect on the lower astral spheres where souls say there is still a night and a day, fog, rain, etc. On the lowest spheres there seems to be deep fog or darkness created by all the negative thoughts and fears of the materialistically minded physical inhabitants of Earth. However, on the mid to higher astral worlds there seems to be a constant "illumination" or "celestial light" source of very soothing, loving, healing radiance of a magical and mysterious nature emanating from "God" and/or the higher realms.

Souls have reported seeing a mysterious, golden light with increasing brightness toward the horizon. I did hear from some of the Leslie Flint recordings, that there are periods of restfulness and twilight but no actual nights except on the lowest spheres where it can get completely dark.

My speculation is that there are probably as many as seven main spheres or heavens (maybe extending hundreds of miles into space?) that are concentric with the earth and rotate along with the physical earth while having no actual boundaries but commingle as one continuous spectrum.

Much of the light enjoyed in the astral spheres probably emanates from the outer chromosphere of the sun as a series or layers of ethereal "suns" expanding beyond, yet concentric with the physical sun and each one illuminating corresponding astral spheres at its own corresponding level of vibration. After the sun sets over the western horizon, much of its outer chromosphere and especially its extended magnetosphere remains above the horizon most of the night, especially toward the upper and lower latitudes, therefore creating an effect of twilight instead of the complete darkness experienced on Earth.

However, the souls also say that the atmospheres of the higher astral spheres extend ever further into space as they increase in vibration, reflecting the sun's rays back onto the planet no matter what time of the night it is with the effect being that of a long twilight during the night rather than complete darkness. There is also a mysterious but very soothing and warm "celestial light" that may souls say replaces the sunlight experienced on Earth and in the lowest spheres. Regardless of where it comes from, the light or illumination in the higher spheres is quite awesome: something much more vibrant and far more beautiful than anything experienced on Earth.

Sri Yukteswar said in Chapter 43 "The Resurrection of Sri Yukteswar" in **Autobiography of a Yogi** by Paramhansa Yogananda that there are numerous astral luminaries or "suns" that illuminate the astral worlds and endless numbers of astral solar systems floating in space. Astral matter tends to be self-luminescent anyway, especially toward the higher spheres where astral material tends to become brighter, lighter, richer, more colorful, dazzling, multi-dimensional, transparent and more enchanting. I would have to say, things go far beyond description at the highest and most dazzling levels which I would refer to as being the mental, causal and celestial spheres.

5.6 - The True Nature of Dark Matter and Dark Energy

These astral spheres are most likely made of what astronomers call "dark matter" and "dark energy" which together constitutes about 26% and 70% respectively of the universe but is invisible to telescopes because it is absolutely transparent, does not interact with material atoms, and gives off no radiation. The remaining 4% is physical matter.

The only way dark matter can be detected by today's astronomers is by observing its gravitational effect on the motions of other objects in space. This "dark matter" seems to have a very strong intergalactic influence essential for keeping galaxies from flying apart. Obviously there are different kinds of matter. Imagine matter out of phase (or synch) with physical matter. Well, most of the matter in the universe appears to be out of phase (invisible and of a different vibration rate) from all the visible matter in our physical universe.

I strongly suspect "dark energy" is an effect of zero point (quantum) energy throughout all space and time, and seems to be responsible for a vast expansive force causing the whole universe to expand in all directions at an accelerating rate. It also seems to be the most original and ultimate source of all the energy in the universe.

5.7 - Does Time Exist in the Afterlife?

The consequences of time as we experience it on Earth do not seem to exist in the afterlife, so no one ever seems to age or have to worry about running out of time. Except on the lowest astral spheres which are still under the influence of earthly rhythms, it seems that spirits can create as much time as they need for any purpose, and are therefore, when in their own environment, always relaxed and never hurried.

Imagine always being able to take as long as you need to to do whatever you want to do and never having to worry about being late! For instance, if one needed a few extra hours when only minutes remained, I speculate that one would simply raise his or her vibration rate and/or retreat into a more timeless (higher) dimension of reality or even go into a state where no time passes at all! In addition to being free of all the limitations of time, there are none of the stressful urgencies, requirements, deadlines, and/or limitations one would often have to deal with while on Earth. It seems that in most of the realms of the afterlife, one can relax and take as long as one needs to relax!

The souls often say that time in their dimension is experienced quite differently. They say there is a form of time, but not measured by the earth's rotation, but more like as an order or sequence of events experienced within one's consciousness which can vary from individual to individual depending on what strata of consciousness and/or sphere or vibration rate one is on.

Time generally seems to be quite a different thing in the afterlife and there seems to be some sort of timelessness, freedom from or transcendence to earthly time which is purely a material thing. The afterlife extends into higher dimensions far beyond the limiting dimensions of the time and space so characteristic of the physical world. The higher the vibrations of the dimension or sphere beyond the physical world, the more and more timeless it seems to get.

My speculation is that time expands at the higher vibrational spheres so that a whole week of information or experiences on the upper spheres could be contained within a few hours of Earth time. It has been said that any clocks built to measure time in the middle to higher spheres of the afterlife simply either stop ticking or don't work at all. Yet at places very near the Earth vibration such as Francisco Xavier's **Nosso Lar** clocks and other timepieces are still manufactured, and can to some extent, still remain accurate enough to be practical.

I speculate that this odd behavior of time in the afterlife can be explained by how the laws of physics and quantum mechanics behave in the afterlife which tend to have a far more liberating influence the higher the sphere or level of consciousness we get. In more rarified regions of higher vibration, the sequential timeline (having 4 dimensions) fans out deeper and ever deeper into probability (having 5 dimensions) so that instead of motion happening as an event along a single timeline, it becomes more and more of a shifting of events into an endless series of possibilities which are typically governed or influenced by thought. In other words consciousness is no longer limited to one timeline, instead it is able to shift through multiple timelines (going past, future and sideways) or through every possible action or probability and on the finest spheres every possible law of physics!

If a spiritually advanced scientific researcher built a "Big Ben" on one of the highest regions of the astral plane, or even an atomic clock for that matter, either the poor device would simply not know which way to go, or it would have to say whatever one's mind makes it up to say! Therefore in the finest of astral realities, I imagine time (having 4 dimensions) must transform more completely to a condition of the mind (having 5 dimensions).

On the very highest spheres space and time as we know them cease to exist. On the finest planes of existence, all of nature expresses as very abstract vibrations of an almost infinite spectrum of astonishing colors, textures and unimaginably beautiful celestial music! Everything merges toward a universal Oneness, perfect beauty or Wholeness.

The higher the strata of consciousness, the higher the vibration, and the further it can go into higher and finer geometric dimensions (5,6,7, etc.). The higher the geometric dimension, the easier it gets for consciousness, energy and matter to merge into a universal, timeless Oneness or Wholeness and the easier it is for a spiritual master to send his consciousness anywhere and view any event in history instantly.

I speculate that on the very highest spheres it might be possible that years and years worth of experience could be had within one or two Earth days or even minutes! Whereas some rather dazed and confused earthbound souls while stuck on some very low vibrational levels may feel that only a few weeks have gone by when actually years of Earth time may have passed. Therefore the experience of time tends to be much more subjective in the afterlife than while living on Earth.

The rate at which one experiences time is really a state of consciousness anyway and nothing more. Souls also seem to have the ability to intuitively sense future events just like some prophets or fortune tellers can on Earth. They can also see back into the past to an extent as well. It is even possible for any soul with the help of a master or adept to go back and experience all the details of actual past historic events which have somehow been recorded in the atmosphere on an etheric level.

The souls say that reality is actually much vaster than just "past, present and future," strongly indicating to me that higher dimension(s) beyond time and space indeed exist and are easily accessed and/or understood by the more advanced souls of the astral planes.

5.8 - Can Distance be Measured in The Astral World?

Distance is never a problem either, as vast distances can be covered within a very short frame of time, simply by closing one's eyes and then concentrating or meditating on a new location for a few moments. No cars, trains or planes are needed although it is possible there could be a few. However, they definitely do have ships, yachts, and other watercraft that are moved about by the power of concentrated willpower or intention, if not astral breezes and water currents, usually piloted by someone who has some experience with that sort of thing.

I am amazed they do have "water" but what it really is I don't really know. By far, most of the time the spirits get around by "physically" walking and in some odd way can also travel great distances in a short period of time just by walking.

In some cases, especially if they need to get from one sphere or level of vibration to another, they must glide or take flight "like Peter Pan" as some souls have compared it to. An intention-guided (quantum) force or energy carries them aloft. In the same way that time is affected by one's state of consciousness, distance also seems to be a much more personal thing, or rather a state of consciousness and/or mind.

Regardless of to what extent the afterlife is a condition of mind, the astral spheres are as real and objective as any reality, if not more so. Astral events and places, especially on the lower spheres can still be objectively timed and mapped.

I'm not saying that the astral spheres don't have a definite geography and logical, objective sequences of time, it's just that all astral distances and lengths of time can be perceived and experienced quite differently from various different "soul" perspectives or angles according to one's degree of evolution, connectedness and familiarity to various locations, and level of awareness or attitude of mind.

There is a kind of objective measurement of time and distance possible in the astral worlds, but depending on which sphere of consciousness one happens to be on, no one needs to be limited by any such thing. There seems to always be a higher way to escape or go outside any so called "physical" measurements or "limitations" that may still exist in the astral worlds. This effect exists because of the availability of higher dimensions in the afterlife.

Part 6 - Astral Projections from the Physical Body

6.1 - Astral Travel (Projection)

What is Astral Projection and What Are the Best Conditions for this Strange Experience? Astral projections are also known as out-of-body experiences and as "soul travel" by some groups, which can happen to anyone at any time in one's life. Astral projections are often confused with lucid or vivid dreaming and skeptics would say that what most people would experience as an out-of-body experience is just a dream.

Even though it is quite common for astral projections to be immediately proceeded by a vivid dream or even be mixed up with or embedded within dreams, when one has a full-blown out-of-body astral experience, it is often so real, so vivid and clear that in no way, shape or form is it considered by the experiencer as just being a dream.

Genuine astral projections are experienced as a fully awakened state outside the body, and the person is able to actually see, usually from a strange angle, his or her still or lifeless looking body lying down on the bed, sofa or couch. One is able to see minute details in the room and travel anywhere else conceivable and watch events and discover new places and/or previously lost or undiscovered items that can later be con firmed.

Certain Tibetan masters and Indian yogi masters throughout history have developed the ability to experience fully conscious astral projections at will and as a result of this awesome faculty, many other special powers too. A contemporary example is Yogiraj Gurunath Siddhanath who because I have met him personally and directly experienced his amazing aura of energy (darshan), I may have seen a few times in the astral as there were some instances of this great yogi's presence appearing during my sleep and in deep meditation.

Other such great masters of astral projection in the past include Rabindranath Tagore who came back speaking through the ectoplasm of direct voice medium, Leslie Flint, regarding his experiences with astral travel and general information on the power of thought; Paramhansa Yogananda, Sri Yukteswar, and the transmigrated Tibetan Lama, Tuesday Lobsang Rampa in the body of Cyril Henry Hoskin. Rampa provided the most outstanding descriptions and knowledge of astral projection, however he was also apparently the author of some of the most controversial books I ever read.

6.2 - The Right Conditions for Astral Projection to Occur

The right conditions for conscious astral projections are tricky to master. To start with it is very helpful to learn meditation and train the body to increase concentration on the inner self (third eye) and withdrawing away from the external senses, while calming down one's breathing and slowing down heart rate toward 40 beats per minute.

Celibacy is quite essential, otherwise it can be challenging trying to maintain the constant enthusiasm and concentration required for the successful completion of this project which involves the process of slowing metabolic rate and fully replacing all physical activity, physical thought, awareness, and consciousness with internal spiritual awareness to the point that the physical becomes quite numb, cold, still and lifeless. Only then in such a deep trance does it become possible to consciously leave the body at will. Such an attainment of this nature is quite profound, vital and priceless, because such an ability leads to a complete mastery over the very powers of life, death and reincarnation.

It is extremely unfortunate that during this present age, the overall tendency of humankind is too much external stimulation, way too much sensual, and too much of one's energy, attention and time is used up by the all the pressures, distractions and responsibilities of the physical world and multiple disturbances through the physical senses. People, especially in this day and age, allow their lives to become far too complicated to seriously commit themselves to exploring the spiritual realms and higher states of consciousness.

It is these overall tendencies to get stuck in sensual and materialistic gratifications and attachments that are causing so much pain, so much skepticism against spiritual truths, confusion and suffering in the world. This grave concern is the main reason why I am taking so much of my time to research and share this information.

Spontaneous astral projections during deep sleep are much more common and more accessible by some. The odds of astral travel occurring during deep sleep can be improved by some form of vigorous physical exercise near the end of the day so that muscles are no longer restless and are therefore more prone to relaxation. In early evening after a light dinner (or sometimes even a fast depending on individual need) one should practice a little yoga and do some meditation before sleeping.

Start actual night time period of rest or sleep with a deep relaxation posture while concentrating on every muscle in the body to completely relax, withdrawing energy from each and every muscle to all the spinal centers and then up to third eye. Try to remain wide-awake while body falls asleep. If this does not work, (usually takes several weeks of practice) set alarm at 3:00 or 4:00 AM, get up and exercise for 15 minutes at that time and then follow the same deep relaxation routine leading to a wide-awake yet fully asleep effect.

What should happen is a deep internalization of awareness along with a state of temporary paralysis (catalepsy) and a terrific vibration and/or intense tingling sensation that can seem way too intense to stand. In this vibrational state, it becomes possible to split away from the body and the further away one gets the less vibration one feels until one is several feet away and some can observe a silver cord between the physical and astral or etheric self.

It becomes possible then to move about the room by concentration on where one wants to go. It takes much practice at first to learn how to control the astral body which is much like the life of a newborn child which has yet to learn how to walk and run, etc.

There is absolutely no danger or ever any real reason to fear astral projection or even death for that matter. If one has to die then death involves simply taking up a much more permanent residence at one's true home in one of the astral spheres. Fear during the first few attempts at astral travel is a huge problem and one will often find oneself slammed right back into the physical body under the slightest provocation of fear and/or even thinking of the physical.

Death can never be caused by astral projection, however the process of dying is often the greatest opportunity ever for astral projection! There are countless worlds in the afterlife that are filled with vast wonders and opportunities of all kinds. For those who are good-natured, kindhearted and full of love (most people are) the afterlife is simply wonderful and filled with unspeakable beauty, great love, awesome bliss, great music and great adventures without any of the time constraints and other limitations that are so much of a problem while living on Earth.

As long as no illicit drugs and/or alcohol are involved, astral projection is a 100% natural, 100% safe and 100% blissful occurrence. Astral projections are an expression of the conscious freedom of the soul while the physical body is in a temporarily state of suspended animation and slowed down or "hibernating" metabolism. The more often one can induce this temporary "death" of the physical, the sooner one becomes an adept or master over the otherwise terrible whims of life and death.

6.3 - Various Forms of Projection: From Clairvoyance

to Complete Immersion

There are various forms of astral projections. The simplest is remote viewing, which really is a form of traveling clairvoyance as a fragment of one's self senses events and scenes from a remote location while the remote viewer sits in a darkened room in a light state of trance.

While meditating in my darkened apartment one morning sometime around 2006, I could actually see within my mind's eye (or third eye?) a clear image of some contractors working on the roof of a small house. It had a chimney and it appeared like there were up to seven contractors working on the construction of a new roof.

At first I assumed I must have been picking up a scene from the astral plane (happens to me sometimes) of astral workers creating an astral building (does happen on some of the astral worlds). It was not until after I stopped meditating, and while on the way to get my mail, I happened to notice a small house going up right next to my apartment complex with the same contractors working on the same roof with chimney, etc!

It is experiences like the above that prove to me beyond a shadow of a doubt about their reality. Experiences of remote viewing, though rare and hard to repeat, are real as day.

A deeper form of remote viewing occurs when the soul is aware in two places at once, behind the physical eyes and from within the astral viewpoint. This effect does happen and illustrates the fact that as long as the physical body remains alive, the soul stays behind with the body while its etheric double goes around and about which the soul also keeps in touch with.

Another form of astral travel is actually the out-of-body experience where one is aware mainly of the etheric counterpart of the earth plane and can perceive, even sometimes feel (but not actually touch or pick up except under very rare conditions), all the things most closely associated with Earth. Actual astral projection is travel in the higher spheres above the earth plane where one is in the astral counterpart (or duplicate) of one's physical body and can meet friends and loved ones who either have passed over or are also asleep, dreaming and/or astral traveling!

There have been some documented cases where one has actually seen while wide awake physically someone else's etheric double (or doppelganger) standing in the same room often to say "goodbye" to a loved one if while in grave danger and/or dying or simply while astral-projecting. In the book, **Autobiography of a Yogi** by Paramhansa Yogananda, there are several instances of yogis traveling in their astral bodies either while still physically living or even after their deaths who were able to fully appear in a solid form in front of various witnesses. For example, read Chapter 43, "The Resurrection of Sri Yukteswar" and wonder about that. Paramhansa Yogananda never had any personal reason(s) or inclinations to ever lie or deceive others.

I personally had someone come visit me in the astral while I was in a deep relaxation trance in my early twenties. This person's energy was so intense it pulled me out of my body through my heart center! Then when I saw this guy sitting with his normal clothes on in a meditation posture right in front of me, I had no idea whatsoever that he was there because he had just died! Here is the whole incident from Chapter 14 of my free, online book, **The Science of Wholeness Part II**:

One weekend in the fall of 1979, I fell asleep alone (I was often tired) in my upstairs bedroom during a meditation/deep relaxation practice. The next thing I knew, my heart chakra was being blasted by an immense power surge. So great was this power surge, it felt like I was hooked up to the entire Edison Power Company and that my chest was the light bulb! I struggled desperately not to explode! It was frightening enough to make me try to wake up out of my trance, but I couldn't.

My heart expanded into a vast white mist in all directions. All I could see was white everywhere. Then I saw my "friend" in most vivid detail sitting in meditation with a smile on his face and surrounded by all this white energy. I sensed some sort of message, something like "we are both spiritual beings, students from the same class, children of the one God." He wasn't exactly someone I knew very well--just a student in one of my classes at Orange Coast College--"Expanded Awareness in Literature"--taught by a rather open-minded English instructor.

When I came out of this strange experience, I thought that maybe this individual, who I knew only briefly, must have been doing some "heavy-duty" meditation at the same time I was and astral-projected to my place. Or why would I have such a strange vision of someone I hardly knew?

Back in class the next week, I received shocking news; the person I saw in my "vision" had died instantly in a terrible motorcycle accident three days before my unusual "meditation" experience. I knew little about him except regarding his interest in Saint Germain and his association with Elizabeth C. Prophet's "Soul Center

Foundation."

Was this strange experience just a coincidence, or did he actually come back from the dead and blast me with an overwhelming surge of white energy while in a deep trance? I know for sure these things are real, and when one has a paranormal experience, there is no denying it whatsoever, it happened!

The wise yogi learns how to calm his breath, slow down his heartbeat and withdraw his physical energy deep into the spinal centers and then ultimately deep into the third eye where he can "die daily" with full ability to leave his body at will just as one can leave one's vehicle by simply opening the door and walking out of it.

The late Indian poet and master of yoga, Rabindranath Tagore, who came back from the spirit realms speaking through the ectoplasm of direct voice medium Leslie Flint, very clearly explains his life-long interest in astral projection and how he mastered it and the unspeakable beauty of the higher spheres that he now lives on.

Unless one has (perhaps in a past life) previously learned it, astral projection is never something one can simply learn overnight and then do for recreation or entertainment. It is rather a serious undertaking requiring total commitment.

Astral projection is a spiritual enrichment practice and not something one should do only for materialistic, sensual, selfish or mundane reasons, as such low levels of intention and/or consciousness would be unwise and make it much harder to achieve any worthwhile results.

6.4 - Two Astral World Experiences I Really Enjoyed

Way back in August 2009, I enjoyed a really amazing and vivid "astral" dream. I might as well share it with you as an example of what can be experienced on an "astral plane" beyond the everyday physical waking experience:

I ascended up through the ceiling, attic and roof of my apartment. On top of the roof, I vividly recall the unique features of a slightly overweight lady on the way up to the "astral plane" who appeared quite well but seemed to indicate her body was not. She seemed like someone I had known in the past and tried to get her name. She said her name very softly; then I could not remember what it was.

I do remember feeling really free and felt like I could walk anywhere and the world around me had transformed into something of a higher sphere or plane of existence.

A cobblestone path winding through a rural neighborhood landscape of parks, trees and natural dwellings materialized out of thin air and ascended before me. I felt like I was embarking on a real adventure in a blissful wonderland similar to "Wizard of Oz." I met and conversed with a few occasional inhabitants on the way up.

I traveled through a hilly landscape with trees, stone walls, and beautiful fabricated "log cabins" and "garden sheds" made from the natural materials (concrete/gravel/mud?) of the surrounding environment. The atmosphere seemed quite rarefied--rather like being on the top of Mt. Everest.

As I finally got to the summit of a very high hill I could see lengthy clouds on the horizon with a perfectly clear pre-dawn sky. It looked as if the sun had not yet come up. The scene unfolded so vividly it startled me, even scared me a little because of my fear of open spaces and heights; the air was pristine and pure, as if I had traveled to another country or even another planet where there was absolutely no pollution whatsoever. The colors were amazingly vivid, especially the trees and plants around me.

I was absolutely excited and ecstatic and extremely interested in the whole experience and tried to get as much information as I could. I felt so good I could not stop smiling and laughing at everything I saw. Whenever I came across anyone, I would ask questions and was directed to visit a particular individual who could really answer my questions and even show me inside his dwelling!

I made my way toward the particular address or location where the fellow lived who would allow me to see inside one of the modest houses which all looked perfectly functional, in order, and complete. All of the dwellings looked like they were made of a whitish mud (thin walls) yet, even though somewhat crooked, were built in a rather modern style with large picture windows, light blinds, etc.

When I reached one of the houses, I could see the person I was looking for standing in the window waving and smiling at me, and calling my name telepathically. A youngish looking man (along with an attractive lady: his wife?) with slightly long blond hair and very neatly cut, short beard stood behind one of the windows. As I tried to enter through the window, it did not allow me to go through and snapped back in my face like a rubber band! Laughing, I thought I obviously should have entered through the door, which I finally did.
Inside the dwelling, everything, including the counter, furniture, wooden cupboards, etc. appeared perfectly

clean and beautiful. The sun, which had now risen, seemed to penetrate all parts of the house inside, illuminating everything in a beautiful way. I noticed actual plumbing and it looked like a normal kitchen sink and all the other houses seemed to have the same sort of accommodations! Utterly fascinated, I went to try and get some water to drink.

I noticed a little repair work needed doing; a screw was loose on one of the faucets as I turned it on. I tried to fix it, laughing hilariously at the thought that even an astral home's water faucets need some maintenance occasionally! The water came out into a perfectly natural looking stainless steel sink and was amazingly pure, pristine, sparkling and beautiful with tiny bubbles in it. I ran some on my hands and tried to drink some of it directly from my hands. What little I had was really amazing because it looked so perfect, so absolutely clean, felt full of vibrant, vibrating life, smelled and tasted absolutely refreshing.

I asked my host to fetch me a glass because I really wanted to drink much more of it! As my host reached for a glass of water from his kitchen cupboard, I asked him to hurry because I felt myself starting to wake up in the physical, and sure enough, the rising sun shone blissfully into my physical window.

After being awake for a few minutes and reflecting back on the dream, it seemed as real as my present waking reality! I was quite disappointed to come back to my body because I had so many experiments I wanted to perform with the water and so many more questions to ask! Such as where does the water come from, how they get their water pressure, and so on.

Unfortunately I could remember only around one-tenth of this experience and rushed to my computer the moment I woke up to type as much of it down as possible before forgetting even more of it. I can now only remember very small portions of it. At the time it seemed as real as day and my most impressive astral projection experience ever, yet now it seems just a fading dream.

An earlier experience I had back in May of 2009 was quite remarkable too. Here is a summary of it:

I experienced the strangest night of my life! Just as I dozed off in that tranquil state between sleep and wakefulness, hands from out of nothing tapped on my back, or started tugging at me or pulling at my fingers, arms and other parts of my body! To my chagrin, some seemed to have lost their sense of what is decent! If they are women, I could go along with that, but with any male entities, I most definitely could not!

Finally, after completely dozing off to sleep, my astral double was pulled entirely out of my body by a group of spirits, some of whom still seemed to exhibit the oddest intentions with no lack of inhibition, nevertheless their actions evolved to the more spiritual and pure, thank goodness, and everything turned out beautifully positive.

I found myself in a marvelously tranquil dark tunnel or mine with a dark blue "sky" at the end. I could see panoramic night scenes of familiar places in my neighborhood from the end of the tunnel which seemed to transform into the entrance of a cave.

More and more spirits (who looked like ordinary people wearing light night clothing such as Hawaiian shirts, pajamas, etc.) started to appear in front of me guiding me into a rather natural looking "cathedral" of sheltered space that looked like it was some sort of "beach" or "cove" inside a huge cavern of dark, brownish volcanic rock. I never before felt so secure and loved, at least not since I was a baby in my mother's arms!

In the center appeared a large naturally constructed circular theater and weird instruments of different sorts were being presented there. Next thing I knew, I was listening to incredibly beautiful, amazingly unique "new age" music with "singing crystal" bowls, gongs, flutes, harps, and lovely changing colored lights ranging from deep red, orange, yellow, lime green, blue and purple hues. It filled me with ecstasy and a loving vibration so deep that It saturated every cell of my body leading me to tears.

Music in the realms beyond the physical is an extremely important part of astral life. It is a time for astral souls to get together in a communion of harmony with each other while obtaining great benefit from the healing and energizing vibrational tones. Actual instruments manufactured from astral materials found in nature are used to vibrate the rarified atmosphere with soothing and emotionally uplifting notes.

The human astral body consists of seven main energy centers or chakras each broadcasting into the universe their own vibrational rate of auric color and therefore attracting and/or creating whatever it gives out. Negative emotions such as anger, frustration and fear are symptoms of vibrational disharmony.

One of the most enjoyable and fastest ways to speed up spiritual evolution and create excellent mental health is through music. The emotional instrument of the astral body needs to be fine-tuned, and one of the best ways is through habitual and continuous listening to the perfectly balanced and harmonious "music of the spheres."

I remembered experiencing various conversations with the astral beings on that side of life. Some looked like people I had known many years ago and all looked relatively young and healthy. I shook many hands and asked some of them if they are members of my group soul and they replied, "not exactly."

I remember looking down and seeing my self wearing black socks and loose clothing. I noticed light colored sand scattered over with pieces of sharp-edged darkly contrasting auburn volcanic rock. I wondered why it did not hurt my feet. The barren cavelike environment with a sandy bottom consisted entirely of volcanic rock, giving me a feeling of a location somewhere near the shoreline of a remote island in the Pacific during the late night hours. Although the place dimly glowed with torches, no light is actually needed because the soul can "see" intuitively. It also seemed strangely familiar.

To my dismay, I could feel myself starting to wake up. Fully aware I was about to leave, many hands waved me good night and I was back in my body, wishing so much I could stay there longer and not have to return to Earth! Upon analysis, I think this experience took place on one of the lower astral planes, because there was no vegetation, everything and everyone looked and acted quite physical, and it was all bare rock, sand and gravel. A skeptic would say it was just a vivid dream which is fine, because dreams are one and the same as the physical brain's interpretation of the spirit's sojourns in the astral world at night which is far more common that one may realize.

Part 7 - Concluding Thoughts

7.1 - Communication With Earth

The inhabitants of the astral worlds and spiritual worlds (mental and causal planes) have always been anxious to communicate with the physical world. Among thousands of reasons one of the most common is the need of one recently passed over to tell immediate relatives and friends of survival.

Globally, there are huge numbers of very wise souls who long to help straighten out all the misconceptions of the afterlife so widely held throughout most of the religions, and to help stamp out materialism, religious bigotry, racial hatred, crime, wars and all other forms of intolerance based on human ignorance.

The spirits long to prove that all living beings everywhere are all children of the same Divine Parent with the same consciousness and of the same breath and that there is no death, only a great new beginning in an eternity of joy and love.

The spirits are fully aware of all the problems of Earth, and have endless insights into how to stop or alleviate all suffering, confusion, fear, and environmental problems, etc. in the physical world. Their love, patience and compassion is almost infinite, and then try to do everything they possibly can to help us.

Their intelligence, knowledge, memory and sense of humor tend to be far greater than beings caught up in the physical body. They are not gods, and are not perfect (still amazingly human!), but they are profoundly talented and capable of incredible things, and are able to see far more (in all ways) than those stuck in the limitations of the physical body and world.

Their contribution to the physical world would be (and already is in certain limited ways) inconceivably immense. Many inventions, creative expressions, etc. throughout history have often come from advanced souls or spirits tuning into and influencing the subconscious minds of various inventors, scientists, artists, etc. on Earth.

Scientists are working on both sides trying to bridge the gap between the physical and spiritual worlds. Much of the research being carried out is controversial, and many of the EVP recordings and photos appear to be just random sounds and images that happen to resemble words, phrases and faces.

However, whenever two-way conversations were

achieved, naturally I followed with great interest all those experiments! One can read and see schematics of how the experiments were carried out and read about the history of all the different methods used to try to establish two-way communication, and one can see that much serious work has been carried out for decades with scientists from both sides.

One of the most successful (yet most credible) examples I have seen so far is the work of Hans Otto Koenig who established two-way conversation using some kind of delicately tuned infrared sender-receiver system which the spirits themselves helped Hans design. The following IR frequencies were given to Hans by the souls: 935.5; 937.8; 927.2; 948.1; 934.2; 928.3 nm (nanometer) to more perfectly adjust the frequencies to the thoughts sent by the spirits.

So why is Hans Otto Koenig not world famous and why were no real follow-ups done on his experiments by mainstream scientists? Continuing progress is likely to be slow until enough scientists take it more seriously. Unfortunately, the majority of mainstream scientists would tend to find this subject too unbelievable and too much of a risk to their credibility, reputation and bank account; even worse, such experiments are hard to duplicate because the "mediumship" factor.

As with almost all the successful communication experiments shown on WorldITC.org there needed to be someone present naturally endowed with a special sort of energy, channel or "mediumship" factor that the spirits must use even with a device, otherwise they would not be able to influence that device at all. This means if a group of skeptical scientists with no mediumship ability whatsoever try to duplicate any of the ITC experiments, it is quite likely they would have no success whatsoever and just call the whole thing a hoax perpetuated by wishful thinking.

No matter how advanced the device constructed, they (the spirits) would most likely still need some sort of mediumship energy to provide some of the connection. The good news is that almost any loving, vital and open-minded person (especially someone very young) can sooner or later develop enough mediumistic energy to provide whatever is needed.

Of course, the most advanced and complete device yet to be invented would have to require either the least amount of "mediumship" factor ever or none at all, and the only way this effect would be possible would be by inventing a method (or chemical mixture) that somehow creates an ever renewable source of its own highly concentrated vital or subtle energy that spirits can use to express themselves with on a physical vibration. In other words, an artificial ectoplasm (rather like artificial insulin) that could be created from the mixture of rather exotic chemicals in a darkened laboratory.

However, in order to avoid the "sorcery" effect of dark entities coming through, one still would need to be careful regarding what sort of intentions one has and to make sure one's level of spirituality is fairly decent. The type and quality of one's own energy and disposition would still be a very serious factor determining or attracting what sort of entities and information comes through.

Things being the way they are, it really is up to people like us to try to support and continue this great work.

The transcendental spheres are created from much higher and finer energies and substances than the physical plane and are not of an electromagnetic source which unfortunately seems entirely confined to physical matter. It is a very challenging problem and much more work needs to be done to make the voices clearer and communication easier. The problem is the spiritual worlds are on completely different "wave lengths" and vibrations than that of physical matter.

It is amazing that any sort of communication takes place

at all. My latest theory on what sort of energy does get through from the astral to the physical is what is known as "torsion field energy" which is what I understand to be gyrational quantum forces (antigravity waves?) caused by the influence of spinning planets, molecules, atoms, electrons, etc. that would somehow speed up or slow down other spinning objects. Astrological influences, homeopathy, telepathy, clairvoyance, levitation, PK energy (telekinesis), prana, and all other paranormal and ESP activity are most likely effects produced by this sort of energy.

Very few scientists are open-minded enough to overcome all the skepticism and prejudice so commonly held against this field of research as spiritualism has unfortunately been associated with all the wrong things by such religions as Christianity, is rejected by mainstream science, and also is ruined and given a bad name by all the countless fakes, flakes, hoaxes and even mischievous spirits themselves.

Even though most souls are extremely good, loving and kind, there are some who are morally deprived and not very evolved and therefore of a low vibration. Special care must be made to avoid those spirits stuck on the lower vibrational spheres because of their bad temperament. Unfortunately, it is important that seances be done in pitch darkness so as to allow ectoplasm to materialize, however a dim red light can be used to help see and photograph ectoplasmic materializations. Much information regarding one of the most complete materializations that was closely studied and confirmed by the English chemist and physicist Sir William Crookes (1832-1919) can be found on the internet. However, conversations with spirits through a spirit communication device will most likely not need to be done in the dark, unless the formation of ectoplasm were part of the design.

7.2 - Epilog: Only the Beginning

It appears that the human being and nearly all other life forms are redundant on many levels of consciousness beyond the physical realm. Unfortunately, mainstream science assumes that the physical world is the only valid existence and therefore systematically rejects any evidence, no matter how obvious or persistent, of paranormal and spiritual phenomena.

There is far more work, organization, universal cooperation and open-minded scientific research (of a selfless nature and made available to all) that needs to be done, especially if more and more scientists are to be convinced of the reality of the afterlife and if its mysteries are to be more fully solved.

Spiritualism is clearly a field of knowledge that has a long way to go before being accepted as a reality by mainstream scientists. Instead, the phenomenon of ectoplasm is still completely rejected and even ridiculed by mainstream academic professors and anyone in high standing showing an interest in such matters would still be in danger of losing their job, funding and/or support.

There is far too much materialistic, academic and religious prejudice yet to cut through before mainstream authorities in this world fully accept spiritualism as a legitimate field of study. Humanity's understanding the true nature of life and the Universe is a never-ending story!

The validity of spiritualism has been proven time and time again. The burden of proof should no longer lie in the laps of those whose main interest is life after death, it is now up to the orthodox theologians and mainstream scientists to become open-minded enough to accept the overwhelming evidence of the paranormal that is freely available in every library and all over the internet. Obviously, and as if to complicate things or make matters worse, there is also plenty of hoaxing, misinterpretation and fictional "evidence" too that one has to sort out from the real evidence.

I accept the paranormal voice recordings in the presence

of Leslie Flint as real evidence because of the sheer volume, consistency, quality, naturalness, and genuine nature of the conversations with multiple witnesses. Even though Leslie Flint passed over in 1994, spiritualist seance recordings by the Australian direct voice medium David Thompson continue to be created and hopefully will remain freely available at the Circle of the Silver Cord website.

Careful listening to the sounds of ectoplasm and study of as many of his seance recordings as I can get a hold of have also convinced me of David's genuine nature. We are really just getting started in the delicate and controversial field of afterlife study and communication and I am sincerely hoping that many more genuine direct voice mediums will continue to illuminate our world of spiritual darkness.

Relevant Websites:

Leslie Flint: http://www.leslieflint.com/

Bashar/Darryl Anka: http://www.bashar.org/

Victor Zammit: http://www.victorzammit.com/

Circle of the Silver Cord: http://circleofthesilvercord.net/

The Author's Websites:

My first website: http://www.wholejoy.com/

My second website: http://www.scienceofwholeness.com

The complete and most up-to-date list of all books by the author: http://wholejoy.com/l/Spiritual-Books.html

References:

Voices in the Dark - Leslie Flint

Autobiography of a Yogi - Paramhansa Yogananda

The Oversoul 7 Triology - Jane Roberts

The Life Elysian - Robert James Lees

Life in the World Unseen - Anthony Borgia

Ultimate Journey - Robert Monroe

Other Books by the Author:

PLEASE GO HERE TO . . .

Discover Sacred, Inspirational and Alternative Healing eBooks by Yogi Shaktivirya

Browse the complete list of all books by the author, Yogi Shaktivirya (Russell Symonds) on Life After Death, Spiritual Nutrition, Spiritual Energy, Law of Attraction, Cosmology, Alternative Healing, Meditation, Breathranianism, Transmutation and many more subjects!

The complete and most up-to-date list of all books by the author: http://wholejoy.com/l/Spiritual-Books.html